A STUDY OF VICTOR HUGO

A STUDY

OF

VICTOR HUGO

BY

ALGERNON CHARLES SWINBURNE

KENNIKAT PRESS
Port Washington, N. Y./London

A STUDY OF VICTOR HUGO

First published in 1886
Reissued in 1970 by Kennikat Press
Library of Congress Catalog Card No: 78-113323
ISBN 0-8046-1000-2

Manufactured by Taylor Publishing Company   Dallas, Texas

PREFACE.

IF the title chosen for this book should be impeached on the score of inaccuracy and presumption, I must admit that it might not seem easy to confute the charge. A full and thorough study of the great master whose name is the crowning glory of the nineteenth century could scarcely be comprised in ten times the space here allotted to a rapid and imperfect survey of so sublime and inexhaustible a subject. My principal aim has been to bring into more prominent relief such aspects of the poet and the man as hitherto, for various worse or better reasons, have found least recognition or least acknowledgment in England. It is on this account, no less than on account of my own conscious inability to say anything unfamiliar to anybody in praise of his great romances, that only a few words have been given to works of world-wide fame, and of a popularity qualified only by the exceptional protests of malignant or obtuse eccentricity. *Notre Dame de Paris* and *Les Misérables* need little more introduction to foreign readers than to French : and as a dramatist Victor Hugo is probably far better known abroad than as a lyric or elegiac or epic or satiric poet. I have no further excuse and no better explanation to offer for such various and serious shortcomings as will probably be detected in a work which at least lays no claim to completeness and makes no pretence to adequacy; but which, if it should ever be found serviceable as an introduction to the study of the greatest writer whom the world has seen since Shakespeare, will have fulfilled the utmost hope and realized the utmost ambition of its author.

THE WORK OF VICTOR HUGO.

In the spring of 1616 the greatest Englishman of all time passed away with no public homage or notice, and the first tributes paid to his memory were prefixed to the miserably garbled and inaccurate edition of his works which was issued seven years later by a brace of players under the patronage of a brace of peers. In the spring of 1885 the greatest Frenchman of all time has passed away amid such universal anguish and passion of regret as never before accompanied the death of the greatest among poets. 'The contrast is of course not wholly due to the incalculable progress of humanity during the two hundred and sixty-nine years which divide the date of our mourning from the date of Shakespeare's death : nor even to the vast superiority of Frenchmen to Englishmen in the quality of generous, just, and reasonable gratitude for the very highest of all benefits that man can confer on mankind. For the greatest poet of this century has been more than such a force of indirect and gradual beneficence as every great writer must needs be. His spiritual service has been in its inmost essence, in its highest development, the service of a healer and a comforter, the work of a redeemer and a prophet. Above all other apostles who have brought us each the glad tidings of his peculiar gospel, the free gifts of his special inspiration, has this one deserved to be called by the most beautiful and tender of all human titles—the son of consolation. His burning wrath and scorn unquenchable were fed with light and heat from the inexhaustible dayspring of his love—a fountain of everlasting and unconsuming fire. We know of no such great poet so good, of no such good man so great in genius : not though Milton and Shelley, our greatest lyric singer and our single epic poet, remain with us for signs and examples of devotion as heroic and self-sacrifice as pure. And therefore it is but simply reasonable that not those alone should mourn for him who have been reared and nurtured on the fruits of his creative spirit : that those also whom he wrought and fought for, but who know him only as their champion and their friend—they that cannot even read him, but remember how he laboured in their cause, that their children might fare otherwise than they—should bear no unequal part in the burden of this infinite and worldwide sorrow.

For us, who from childhood upwards have fostered and fortified whatever of good was born in us—all capacity of spiritual work, all seed of human sympathy, all powers of hope and faith, all passions and aspirations found loyal to the service of duty and of love—with the bread of his deathless word and the wine of his immortal song, the one thing possible to do in this first hour of bitterness and stupefaction at the sense of a loss not possible yet to realize is not to declaim his praise or parade our lamentation in modulated effects or efforts of panegyric or of dirge : it is to reckon up once more the standing account of our all but incalculable debt. A brief and simple summary of his published works may probably lay before the student some points and some details not generally familiar to the run of English readers : and I know not what better service might be done them than to bring into their sight such aspects of the most multiform and many-sided genius that ever wrough in prose or verse as are least obvious and least notorious to the foreign world of letters.

Poet, dramatist, novelist, historian, philosopher, and patriot, the spiritual sovereign of the nineteenth century was before all things and above all things a poet. Throughout all the various and ambitious attempts of his marvellous boyhood—criticism, drama, satire, elegy, epigram, and romance —the dominant vein is poetic. His example will stand for ever as the crowning disproof of the doubtless more than plausible opinion that the most amazing precocity of power is a sign of ensuing impotence and premature decay. There was never a more brilliant boy than Victor Hugo : but there has never been a greater man. At any other than a time of mourning it might be neither unseasonable nor unprofitable to observe that the boy's early verse, moulded on the models of the eighteenth century, is an arsenal of satire on revolutionary principles or notions which might suffice to furnish forth with more than their natural equipment of epigram a whole army of reactionary rhymesters and pamphleteers. But from the first, without knowing it, he was on the road to Damascus : if not to be struck down by sudden miracle, yet by no less inevitable a process to undergo a no less unquestionable conversion. At sixteen he wrote for a wager in the space of a fortnight the chivalrous and heroic story of *Bug-Jargal*; afterwards recast and reinformed with fresh vigour of vitality, when the author had attained the maturer age of twenty-three. His tenderness and manliness of spirit were here made nobly manifest : his originality and ardour of imagination, wild as yet and crude and violent, found vent two years later in *Han d'Islande*. But no boyish work on record ever showed more singular force of hand, more brilliant variety of power : though the author's criticism ten years later admits that 'il n'y a dans *Han d'Islande* qu'une chose sentie, l'amour du jeune homme ; qu'une chose observée, l'amour de la jeune fille.' But as the work of a boy's fancy or invention, touched here and there with genuine humour, terror, and pathos, it is not less wonderful than are the author's first odes for ease and force and freshness and fluency of verse imbued with simple and sincere feeling, with cordial and candid faith. And in both these boyish stories the hand of a soldier's son, a child of the camp, reared in the lap of war and cradled in traditions of daring, is evident whenever an episode of martial adventure comes in among the more fantastic excursions of adolescent inventiveness. But it is in the ballads written between his twenty-second and his twenty-seventh year that Victor Hugo first showed himself, beyond all question and above all cavil, an original and a great poet. *La Chasse du Burgrave* and *Le Pas d'Armes du Roi Jean* would suffice of themselves to establish that. The fire, the music, the force, the tenderness, the spirit of these glorious little poems must needs, one would think, impres even such readers as might be impervious to the charm of their exquisitely vigorous and dexterous execution. Take for example this one stanza from the ballad last mentioned :—

> La cohue,
> Flot de fer,
> Frappe, hue,
> Remplit l'air,

Et, profonde,
Tourne et gronde
Comme une onde
Sur la mer.

It will of course, I should hope, be understood once for all that when I venture to select for special mention any special poem of Hugo's I do not dream of venturing to suggest that others are not or may not be fully as worthy of homage, or that anything of this incomparable master's work will not requite our study or does not demand our admiration; I do but take leave to indicate in passing some of those which have been to me especially fruitful of enduring delight, and still are cherished in consequence with a peculiar gratitude.

At twenty-five the already celebrated lyric poet published his magnificent historic drama of *Cromwell* : a work sufficient of itself to establish the author's fame for all ages in which poetry and thought, passion and humour, subtle truth of character, stately perfection of structure, facile force of dialogue and splendid eloquence of style, continue to be admired and enjoyed. That the author has apparently confounded one earl of Rochester with another more famous bearer of the same title must not be allowed to interfere with the credit due to him for wide and various research. Any dullard can point the finger at a slip here and there in the history, a change or an error of detail or of date : it needs more care to appreciate the painstaking and ardent industry which has collected and fused together a great mass of historic and legendary material, the fervent energy of inspiration which has given life, order, and harmony to the vast and versatile design. As to the executive part of the poem, the least that can be said by any competent judge of that

matter is that Molière was already equalled and Corneille
was already excelled in their respective provinces of verse
by the young conqueror whose rule was equal and imperial
over every realm of song. The comic interludes or episodes
of the second and third acts, so admirably welded into the
structure or woven into the thread of the action, would suffice
to prove this when collated with the seventeenth scene of
the third act and the great speech of Cromwell in the fifth.

> Arrêtez !
>
> Que veut dire ceci ?   Pourquoi cette couronne ?
> Que veut-on que j'en fasse ? et qui donc me la donne ?
> Est-ce un rêve ?   Est-ce bien le bandeau que je vois ?
> De quel droit me vient-on confondre avec les rois ?
> Qui mêle un tel scandale à nos pieuses fêtes ?
> Quoi ! leur couronne, à moi qui fais tomber leurs têtes !
> S'est-on mépris au but de ces solennités ?—
> Milords, messieurs, anglais, frères, qui m'écoutez,
> Je ne viens point ici ceindre le diadème,
> Mais retremper mon titre au sein du peuple même,
> Rajeunir mon pouvoir, renouveler mes droits.
> L'écarlate sacrée était teinte deux fois.
> Cette pourpre est au peuple, et, d'une âme loyale,
> Je la tiens de lui.—Mais la couronne royale !
> Quand l'ai-je demandée ?   Et qui dit que j'en veux ?
> Je ne donnerais pas un seul de mes cheveux,
> De ces cheveux blanchis à servir l'Angleterre,
> Pour tous les fleurons d'or des princes de la terre.
> Otez cela d'ici !   Remportez, remportez
> Ce hochet, ridicule entre les vanités !
> N'attendez pas qu' aux pieds je foule ces misères !
> Qu'ils me connaissent mal, les hommes peu sincères
> Qui m'osent affronter jusqu'à me couronner !
> J'ai reçu de Dieu plus qu'ils ne peuvent donner,
> La grâce inamissible ; et de moi je suis maître.
> Une fois fils du ciel, peut-on cesser de l'être ?

De nos prospérités l'univers est jaloux.
Que me faut-il de plus que le bonheur de tous ?
Je vous l'ai dit.   Ce peuple est le peuple d'élite.
L'Europe de cette île est l'humble satellite.
Tout cède à notre étoile ; et l'impie est maudit.
Il semble, à voir cela, que le Seigneur ait dit :
—Angleterre ! grandis, et sois ma fille aînée.
Entre les nations mes mains t'ont couronnée ;
Sois donc ma bien-aimée, et marche à mes côtés.—
Il déroule sur nous d'abondantes bontés ;
Chaque jour qui finit, chaque jour qui commence,
Ajoute un anneau d'or à cette chaîne immense.
On croirait que ce Dieu, terrible aux philistins,
A comme un ouvrier composé nos destins ;
Que son bras, sur un axe indestructible aux âges,
De ce vaste édifice a scellé les rouages,
Œuvre mystérieuse, et dont ses longs efforts
Pour des siècles peut-être ont monté les ressorts.
Ainsi tout va.   La roue, à la roue enchaînée,
Mord de sa dent de fer la machine entraînée ;
Les massifs balanciers, les antennes, les poids,
Labyrinthe vivant, se meuvent à la fois ;
L'effrayante machine accomplit sans relâche
Sa marche inexorable et sa puissante tâche ;
Et des peuples entiers, pris dans ses mille bras,
Disparaîtraient broyés, s'ils ne se rangeaient pas.
Et j'entraverais Dieu, dont la loi salutaire
Nous fait un sort à part dans le sort de la terre !
J'irais, du peuple élu foulant le droit ancien,
Mettre mon intérêt à la place du sien !
Pilote, j'ouvrirais la voile aux vents contraires !

(Hochant la tête.)

Non, je ne donne pas cette joie aux faux frères.
Le vieux navire anglais est toujours roi des flots.
Le colosse est debout.   Que sont d'obscurs complots
Contre les hauts destins de la Grande-Bretagne ?
Qu'est-ce qu'un coup de pioche aux flancs d'une montagne ?

(Promenant des yeux de lynx autour de lui.)

Avis aux malveillants ! on sait tout ce qu'ils font.
Le flot est transparent, si l'abîme est profond.
On voit le fond du piége où rampe leur pensée.
La vipère parfois de son dard s'est blessée ;
Au feu qu'on allumait souvent on se brûla ;
Et les yeux du Seigneur vont courant çà et là.—
Qui du peuple et des rois a signé le divorce ?
Moi.—Croit-on donc me prendre à cette vaine amorce ?
Un diadème !—Anglais, j'en brisais autrefois.
Sans en avoir porté, j'en connais bien le poids.
Quitter pour une cour le camp qui m'environne ?
Changer mon glaive en sceptre et mon casque en couronne ?
Allons ! suis-je un enfant ? me croit-on né d'hier ?
Ne sais-je pas que l'or pèse plus que le fer ?
M'édifier un trône ! Eh ! c'est creuser ma tombe.
Cromwell, pour y monter, sait trop comme on en tombe.
Et d'ailleurs, que d'ennuis s'amassent sur ces fronts
Qui se rident sitôt, hérissés de fleurons !
Chacun de ces fleurons cache une ardente épine
La couronne les tue ; un noir souci les mine ;
Elle change en tyran le mortel le plus doux,
Et, pesant sur le roi, le fait peser sur tous.
Le peuple les admire, et, s'abdiquant lui-même,
Compte tous les rubis dont luit le diadème ;
Mais comme il frémirait pour eux de leur fardeau,
S'il regardait le front et non pas le bandeau !
Eux, leur charge les trouble, et leurs mains souveraines
De l'état chancelant mêlent bientôt les rênes.—
Ah ! remportez ce signe exécrable, odieux !
Ce bandeau trop souvent tombe du front aux yeux.—
              (*Larmoyant.*)
Et qu'en ferais-je enfin ? Mal né pour la puissance,
Je suis simple de cœur et vis dans l'innocence.
Si j'ai, la fronde en main, veillé sur le bercail,
Si j'ai devant l'écueil pris place au gouvernail,
J'ai dû me dévouer pour la cause commune.
Mais que n'ai-je vieilli dans mon humble fortune !

Que n'ai-je vu tomber les tyrans aux abois,
A l'ombre de mon chaume et de mon petit bois !
Hélas ! j'eusse aimé mieux ces champs où l'on respire,
Le ciel m'en est témoin, que les soins de l'empire ;
Et Cromwell eût trouvé plus de charme cent fois
A garder ses moutons qu'à détrôner des rois !
(*Pleurant.*)
Que parle-t-on de sceptre ?   Ah ! j'ai manqué ma vie.
Ce morceau de clinquant n'a rien qui me convie.
Ayez pitié de moi, frères, loin d'envier
Votre vieux général, votre vieil Olivier.
Je sens mon bras faiblir, et ma fin est prochaine.
Depuis assez longtemps suis-je pas à la chaîne ?
Je suis vieux, je suis las ; je demande merci.
N'est-il pas temps qu'enfin je me repose aussi ?
Chaque jour j'en appelle à la bonté divine,
Et devant le Seigneur je frappe ma poitrine.
Que je veuille être roi !   Si frêle et tant d'orgueil !
Ce projet, et j'en jure à côté du cercueil,
Il m'est plus étranger, frères, que la lumière
Du soleil à l'enfant dans le sein de sa mère !
Loin ce nouveau pouvoir à mes vœux présenté !
Je n'en accepte rien,—rien que l'hérédité.

The subtlety and variety of power displayed in the treatment of the chief character should be evident alike to those who look only on the upright side of it and those who can see only its more oblique aspect.   The Cromwell of Hugo is as far from the faultless monster of Carlyle's creation and adoration as from the all but unredeemed villain of royalist and Hibernian tradition : he is a great and terrible poetic figure, imbued throughout with active life and harmonized throughout by imaginative intuition : a patriot and a tyrant, a dissembler and a believer, a practical humourist and a national hero.

The famous preface in which the batteries of pseudoclassic tradition were stormed and shattered at a charge has itself long since become a classic. That the greatest poet was also the greatest prose-writer of his generation there could no longer be any doubt among men of any intelligence : but not even yet was more than half the greatness of his multitudinous force revealed. Two years later, at the age of twenty-seven, he published the superb and entrancing *Orientales* : the most musical and many-coloured volume of verse that ever had glorified the language. From *Le Feu du Ciel* to *Sara la Baigneuse*, from the thunder-peals of exterminating judgment to the flute-notes of innocent girlish luxury in the sense of loveliness and life, the inexhaustible range of his triumph expands and culminates and extends. Shelley has left us no more exquisite and miraculous piece of lyrical craftsmanship than *Les Djinns* ; none perhaps so rich in variety of modulation, so perfect in rise and growth and relapse and reiterance of music.

> Murs, ville,
> Et port,
> Asile
> De mort,
> Mer grise
> Où brise
> La brise,
> Tout dort.
>
> Dans la plaine
> Naît un bruit.
> C'est l'haleine
> De la nuit.
> Elle brame
> Comme une âme
> Qu'une flamme
> Toujours suit.

Then the terrible music of the flight of evil spirits—'trou-
peau lourd et rapide'—grows as it were note by note and
minute by minute up to its full height of tempest, and
again relapses and recedes into the subsiding whisper of the
corresponsive close.

> Ce bruit vague
> Qui s'endort,
> C'est la vague
> Sur le bord ;
> C'est la plainte
> Presque éteinte
> D'une sainte
> Pour un mort.
>
> On doute
> La nuit . . .
> J'écoute :—
> Tout fuit,
> Tout passe ;
> L'espace
> Efface
> Le bruit.

And here, like Shelley, was Hugo already the poet of
freedom, a champion of the sacred right and the holy duty
of resistance.   The husk of a royalist education, the crust of
reactionary misconceptions, had already begun to drop off :
not yet a pure republican, he was now ripe to receive and
to understand the doctrine of human right, the conception
of the common weal, as distinguished from imaginary duties
and opposed to hereditary claims.

The twenty-eighth year of his life, which was illuminated
by the issue of these passionate and radiant poems, witnessed
also the opening of his generous and lifelong campaign or

crusade against the principle of capital punishment. With
all possible reverence and all possible reluctance, but re-
membering that without perfect straightforwardness and
absolute sincerity I should be even unworthier than I am to
speak of Victor Hugo at all, I must say that his reasoning on
this subject seems to me insufficient and inconclusive : that
his own radical principle, the absolute inviolability of human
life, the absolute sinfulness of retributive bloodshedding, if
not utterly illogical and untenable, is tenable or logical only
on the ground assumed by those quaintest though not least
pathetic among fanatics and heroes, the early disciples of
George Fox.   If a man tells you that supernatural revelation
has forbidden him to take another man's life under all and
any circumstances, he is above or beyond refutation : if he
says that self-defence is justifiable, and that righteous war-
fare is a patriotic duty, but that to exact from the very
worst of murderers, a parricide or a poisoner, a Philip the
Second or a Napoleon the Third, the payment of a life for a
life—or even of one infamous existence for whole hecatombs
of innocent lives—is an offence against civilization and a
sin against humanity, I am not merely unable to accept but
incompetent to understand his argument.   We may most
heartily agree with him that France is degraded by the
guillotine, and that England is disgraced by the gallows, and
yet our abhorrence of these barbarous and nauseous bru-
talities may not preclude us from feeling that a dealer (for
example) in professional infanticide by starvation might very
properly be subjected to vivisection without anæsthetics, and
that all manly and womanly minds not distorted or distracted
by prepossessions or assumptions might rationally and laud-
ably rejoice in the prospect of this legal and equitable

process. 'The senseless old law of retaliation' (*la vieille et inepte loi du talion*) is inept or senseless only when the application of it is false to the principle : when justice in theory becomes unjust in practice. Another stale old principle or proverb—'abusus non tollit usum'—suffices to confute some of the arguments—I am very far from saying, all—adduced or alleged by the ardent eloquence of Victor Hugo in his admirable masterpiece of terrible and pathetic invention, *Le dernier jour d'un condamné*, and subsequently in the impressive little history of *Claude Gueux*, in the famous speech on behalf of Charles Hugo when impeached on a charge of insult to the laws in an article on the punishment of death, and in the fervent eloquence of his appeal on the case of a criminal executed in Guernsey, and of his protest addressed to Lord Palmerston against the horrible result of its rejection. That certain surviving methods of execution are execrable scandals to the country which maintains them, he has proved beyond all humane or reasonable question : and that all murderers are not alike inexcusable is no less indisputable a proposition : but beyond these two points the most earnest and exuberant advocacy can advance nothing likely to convince any but those already converted to the principle that human life must never be taken in punishment of crime—that there are not criminals whose existence insults humanity, and cries aloud on justice for mercy's very sake to cut it off.

　　The next year (1830) is famous for ever beyond all others in the history of French literature : it was the year of *Hernani*, the date of liberation and transfiguration for the tragic stage ✓ of France. The battle which raged round the first acted play of Hugo's and the triumph which crowned the struggles

of its champions, are not these things written in too many
chronicles to be for the thousandth time related here ?   And
of its dramatic and poetic quality what praise could be uttered
that must not before this have been repeated at least some
myriads of times?   But if there be any mortal to whom the
heroic scene of the portraits, the majestic and august mono-
logue of Charles the Fifth at the tomb of Charles the Great,
the terrible beauty, the vivid pathos, the bitter sweetness of
the close, convey no sense of genius and utter no message
of delight, we can only say that it would simply be natural,
consistent, and proper for such a critic to recognize in
Shakespeare a barbarian, and a Philistine in Milton.

Nevertheless, if we are to obey the perhaps rather
childish impulse of preference and selection among the
highest works of the highest among poets, I will avow that
to my personal instinct or apprehension *Marion de Lorme* /
seems a yet more perfect and pathetic masterpiece than
even *Hernani* itself.   The always generous and loyal Dumas
placed it at the very head of his friend's dramatic works.
Written, as most readers (I presume) will remember, before
its predecessor on the stage, it was prohibited on the in-
sanely fatuous pretext that the presentation of King Louis
the Thirteenth was an indirect affront to the majesty of King
Charles the Tenth.   After that luckless dotard had been
driven off his throne, it was at once proposed to produce
the hitherto interdicted play before an audience yet palpi-
tating with the thrill of revolution and resentment.   But
the chivalrous loyalty of Victor Hugo refused to accept a
facile and factitious triumph at the expense of an exiled old
man, over the ruins of a shattered old cause.   The play
was not permitted by its author to enter till the spring of

the following year on its inevitable course of glory. It is a curious and memorable fact that the most tender-hearted of all great poets had originally made the hero of this tragedy leave the heroine unforgiven for the momentary and reluctant relapse into shame by which she had endeavoured to repurchase his forfeited life ; and that Prosper Mérimée should have been the first, Marie Dorval the second, to reclaim a little mercy for the penitent. It is to their pleading that we owe the sublime pathos of the final parting between Marion and Didier.

In one point it seems to me that this immortal masterpiece may perhaps be reasonably placed, with *Le Roi s'amuse* and *Ruy Blas*, in triune supremacy at the head of Victor Hugo's plays. The wide range of poetic abilities, the harmonious variety of congregated powers, displayed in these three great tragedies through almost infinite variations of terror and pity and humour and sublime surprise, will seem to some readers, whose reverence is no less grateful for other gifts of the same great hand, unequalled at least till the advent in his eighty-first year of *Torquemada.*

Victor Hugo was not yet thirty when all these triumphs lay behind him. In the twenty-ninth year of a life which would seem fabulous and incredible in the record of its achievements if divided by lapse of time from all possible proof of its possibility by the attestation of dates and facts, he published in February *Notre-Dame de Paris*, in November *Les Feuilles d'Automne* : that the two dreariest months of the year might not only 'smell April and May,' but outshine July and August. The greatest of all tragic romances has a Grecian perfection of structure, with a Gothic intensity of pathos. To attempt the praise of such a work would be only less idle than to refuse it. Terror and pity, with eternal fate for key-note to the strain of story, never struck deeper to men's hearts through more faultless evolution of combining circumstance on the tragic stage of Athens. Louis the Eleventh has been painted by many famous hands, but Hugo's presentation of him, as compared for example with Scott's, is as a portrait by Velasquez to a portrait by Vandyke. The style was a new revelation of the supreme capacities of human speech : the touch of it on any subject of description or of passion is as the touch of the sun for penetrating irradiation and vivid evocation of life.

From the *Autumn Leaves* to the *Songs of the Twilight*, and again from the *Inner Voices* to the *Sunbeams and Shadows*, the continuous jet of lyric song through a space of ten fertile years was so rich in serene and various beauty that the one thing notable in a flying review of its radiant course is the general equality of loveliness in form and colour, which is relieved and heightened at intervals by some especial example of a beauty more profound or more sublime. The first volume of the four, if I mistake not, won a more immediate and universal homage than the rest : its unsurpassed melody was so often the raiment of emotion which struck home to all hearts a sense of domestic tenderness too pure and sweet and simple for perfect expression by any less absolute and omnipotent lord of style, that it is no wonder if in many minds—many mothers' minds especially—there should at once have sprung up an all but ineradicable conviction that no subsequent verse must be allowed to equal or excel the volume which contained such flowerlike jewels of song as the nineteenth and twentieth of

these unwithering and imperishable *Leaves*. But no error
possible to a rational creature could be more serious or
more complete than the assumption of any inferiority in the
volume containing the two glorious poems addressed to
Admiral Canaris, the friend (may I be forgiven the filial
vanity or egotism which impels me to record it?) of the present
writer's father in his youth ; the two first in date of Hugo's
finest satires, the lines that scourge a backbiter and the lines
that brand a traitor (the resonant and radiant indignation of
the latter stands unsurpassed in the very *Châtiments* themselves) ; the two most enchanting aubades or songs of sunrise that ever had outsung the birds and outsweetened the
flowers of the dawn ; and—for here I can cite no more—
the closing tribute of lines more bright than the lilies whose
name they bear, offered by a husband's love at the sweet
still shrine of motherhood and wifehood. The first two
stanzas of the second aubade are all that can here be quoted.

> L'aurore s'allume,
> L'ombre épaisse fuit ;
> Le rêve et la brume
> Vont où va la nuit ;
> Paupières et roses
> S'ouvrent demi-closes ;
> Du réveil des choses
> On entend le bruit.
>
> Tout chante et murmure,
> Tout parle à la fois,
> Fumée et verdure,
> Les nids et les toits ;
> Le vent parle aux chênes,
> L'eau parle aux fontaines ;
> Toutes les haleines
> Deviennent des voix.

And in each of the two succeeding volumes there is, among all their other things of price, a lyric which may even yet be ranked with the highest subsequent work of its author for purity of perfection, for height and fullness of note, for music and movement and informing spirit of life. We ought to have in English, but I fear—or rather I am only too sure—we have not, a song in which the sound of the sea is rendered as in that translation of the trumpet-blast of the night-wind, with all its wails and pauses and fluctuations and returns, done for once into human speech and interpreted into spiritual sense for ever. For instinctive mastery of its means and absolute attainment of its end, for majesty of living music and fidelity of sensitive imagination, there is no lyric poem in any language more wonderful or more delightful.

UNE NUIT QU'ON ENTENDAIT LA MER SANS LA VOIR.

Quels sont ces bruits sourds ?
Écoutez vers l'onde
Cette voix profonde
Qui pleure toujours
Et qui toujours gronde,
Quoiqu'un son plus clair
Parfois l'interrompe . . .—
Le vent de la mer
Souffle dans sa trompe.

Comme il pleut ce soir !
N'est-ce pas, mon hôte ?
Là-bas, à la côte,
Le ciel est bien noir,
La mer est bien haute !

On dirait l'hiver ;
Parfois on s'y trompe . . .—
Le vent de la mer
Souffle dans sa trompe.

Oh ! marins perdus !
Au loin, dans cette ombre,
Sur la nef qui sombre,
Que de bras tendus
Vers la terre sombre !
Pas d'ancre de fer
Que le flot ne rompe.—
Le vent de la mer
Souffle dans sa trompe.

Nochers imprudents !
Le vent dans la voile
Déchire la toile
Comme avec les dents !
Là-haut pas d'étoile !
L'un lutte avec l'air,
L'autre est à la pompe.—
Le vent de la mer
Souffle dans sa trompe.

C'est toi, c'est ton feu
Que le nocher rêve,
Quand le flot s'élève,
Chandelier que Dieu
Pose sur la grève,
Phare au rouge éclair
Que la brume estompe !—
Le vent de la mer
Souffle dans sa trompe.

A yet sweeter and sadder and more magical sea-song there was yet to come years after—but only from the lips of an exile.   Of the ballad—so to call it, if any term of definition may suffice—which stands out as a crowning splendour among *Les Rayons et les Ombres*, not even Hugo's own elo-quence, had it been the work (which is impossible) of any other great poet in all time, could have said anything ade-quate at all.   Not even Coleridge and Shelley, the sole twin sovereigns of English lyric poetry, could have produced this little piece of lyric work by combination and by fusion of their gifts.   The pathetic truthfulness and the simple man-fulness of the mountain shepherd's distraction and devotion might have been given in ruder phrase and tentative render-ing by the nameless ballad-makers of the border : but here is a poem which unites something of the charm of *Clerk Saunders* and *The Wife of Usher's Well* with something of the magic of *Christabel* and the *Ode to the West Wind :* a thing, no doubt, impossible ; but none the less obviously accomplished.[1]

[1] In the winter of the year which in spring had seen *Les Rayons et les Ombres* come forth to kindle and refresh the hearts of readers, Victor Hugo published an ode in the same key as those *To the Column* and *To the Arch of Triumph*, on the return and reinterment of the dead Napoleon.   Full of noble feeling and sonorous eloquence, the place of this poem in any collection of its author's works is distinctly and un-mistakably marked out by every quality it has and by every quality it wants.   In style and in sentiment, in opinion and in rhythm, it is one with the national and political poems which had already been published by the author since the date of his *Orientales* : in other words, it is in every possible point utterly and absolutely unlike the poems long after-wards to be written by the author in exile.   Its old place, therefore, in all former editions, at the end of the volume containing the poems previously published in the same year, is obviously the only right one, and rationally the only one possible.   By what inexplicable and incon-ceivable caprice it has been promoted to a place, in the so-called *édition définitive*, on the mighty roll of the *Légende des Siècles*, at the head of the fourth volume of that crowning work of modern times, I am hopelessly and helplessly at a loss to conjecture.   But, at all risk of impeachment on

The lyric work of these years would have been enough for the energy of another man, for the glory of another poet ; it was but a part, it was (I had wellnigh said) the lesser part, of its author's labours—if labour be not an improper term for the successive or simultaneous expressions or effusions of his indefatigable spirit. The year after *Notre-Dame de Paris* and *Les Feuilles d'Automne* appeared one of the great crowning tragedies of all time, *Le Roi s'amuse.* As the key-note of *Marion de Lorme* had been redemption by expiation, so the key-note of this play is expiation by retribution. The simplicity, originality, and straightforwardness of the terrible means through which this austere conception is worked out would give moral and dramatic value to a work less rich in the tenderest and sublimest poetry, less imbued with the purest fire of pathetic passion. After the magnificent pleading of the Marquis de Nangis in the preceding play, it must have seemed impossible that the poet should without a touch of repetition or reiterance be able again to confront a young king with an old servant, pour forth again the denunciation and appeal of a breaking heart, clothe again the haughtiness of honour, the loyalty of grief, the sanctity of indignation, in words that shine like lightning and verses that thunder like the sea. But the veteran interceding for a nephew's life is a less tragic figure than he who comes to ask account for a daughter's honour. Hugo never merely repeats himself : his miraculous fertility and force of utterance were not more indefatigable and inexhaustible

a charge of unbecoming presumption, I must and do here enter my most earnest and strenuous protest against the claim of an edition to be in any sense final and unalterable, which rejects from among the *Châtiments* the poem on the death of Saint-Arnaud and admits into the *Légende des Siècles* the poem on the reinterment of Napoleon.

than the fountains of thought and emotion which fed that eloquence with fire.

In the seventh scene of the fourth act of *Marion de Lorme*, an old warrior of the days of Henri Quatre comes to plead with the son of his old comrade in arms for the life of his heir, condemned to death as a duellist by the edict of Richelieù.

LE MARQUIS DE NANGIS (*se relevant*).

Je dis qu'il est bien temps que vous y songiez, sire ;
Que le cardinal-duc a de sombres projets,
Et qu'il boit le meilleur du sang de vos sujets.
Votre père Henri, de mémoire royale,
N'eût pas ainsi livré sa noblesse loyale ;
Il ne la frappait point sans y fort regarder ;
Et, bien gardé par elle, il la savait garder.
Il savait qu'on peut faire avec des gens d'épées
Quelque chose de mieux que des têtes coupées ;
Qu'ils sont bons à la guerre. Il ne l'ignorait point,
Lui dont plus d'une balle a troué le pourpoint.
Ce temps était le bon. J'en fus, et je l'honore.
Un peu de seigneurie y palpitait encore.
Jamais à des seigneurs un prêtre n'eût touché.
On n'avait point alors de tête à bon marché.
Sire ! en des jours mauvais comme ceux où nous sommes,
Croyez un vieux, gardez un peu de gentilshommes.
Vous en aurez besoin peut-être à votre tour.
Hélas ! vous gémirez peut-être quelque jour
Que la place de Grève ait été si fêtée,
Et que tant de seigneurs de bravoure indomptée,
Vers qui se tourneront vos regrets envieux,
Soient morts depuis longtemps qui ne seraient pas vieux !
Car nous sommes tout chauds de la guerre civile,
Et le tocsin d'hier gronde encor dans la ville.
Soyez plus ménager des peines du bourreau.
C'est lui qui doit garder son estoc au fourreau,

Non pas vous.   D'échafauds montrez-vous économe.
Craignez d'avoir un jour à pleurer tel brave homme,
Tel vaillant de grand cœur, dont, à l'heure qu'il est,
Le squelette blanchit aux chaînes d'un gibet !
Sire ! le sang n'est pas une bonne rosée ;
Nulle moisson ne vient sur la Grève arrosée,
Et le peuple des rois évite le balcon,
Quand aux dépens du Louvre on peuple Montfaucon.
Meurent les courtisans, s'il faut que leur voix aille
Vous amuser, pendant que le bourreau travaille !
Cette voix des flatteurs qui dit que tout est bon,
Qu'après tout on est fils d'Henri Quatre, et Bourbon,
Si haute qu'elle soit, ne couvre pas sans peine
Le bruit sourd qu'en tombant fait une tête humaine.
Je vous en donne avis, ne jouez pas ce jeu,
Roi, qui serez un jour face à face avec Dieu.
Donc, je vous dis, avant que rien ne s'accomplisse,
Qu'à tout prendre il vaut mieux un combat qu'un supplice,
Que ce n'est pas la joie et l'honneur des états
De voir plus de besogne aux bourreaux qu'aux soldats,
Que c'est un pasteur dur pour la France où vous êtes
Qu'un prêtre qui se paye une dîme de têtes,
Et que cet homme illustre entre les inhumains
Qui touche à votre sceptre—a du sang à ses mains !

In the fifth scene of the first act of *Le Roi s'amuse,* an
old nobleman whose life, forfeit on a charge of friendship or
relationship with rebels, has been repurchased by his daughter
from the king at the price of her honour, is insulted by the
king's jester when he comes to speak with the king, and
speaks thus, without a glance at the jester.

Une insulte de plus !—Vous, sire, écoutez-moi,
Comme vous le devez, puisque vous êtes roi !
Vous m'avez fait un jour mener pieds nus en Grève ;
Là, vous m'avez fait grâce, ainsi que dans un rêve,

Et je vous ai béni, ne sachant en effet
Ce qu'un roi cache au fond d'une grâce qu'il fait.
Or, vous aviez caché ma honte dans la mienne.—
Oui, sire, sans respect pour une race ancienne,
Pour le sang de Poitiers, noble depuis mille ans,
Tandis que, revenant de la Grève à pas lents,
Je priais dans mon cœur le Dieu de la victoire
Qu'il vous donnât mes jours de vie en jours de gloire,
Vous, François de Valois, le soir du même jour,
Sans crainte, sans pitié, sans pudeur, sans amour,
Dans votre lit, tombeau de la vertu des femmes,
Vous avez froidement, sous vos baisers infâmes,
Terni, flétri, souillé, déshonoré, brisé
Diane de Poitiers, comtesse de Brézé !
Quoi ! lorsque j'attendais l'arrêt qui me condamne,
Tu courais donc au Louvre, ô ma chaste Diane !
Et lui, ce roi sacré chevalier par Bayard,
Jeune homme auquel il faut des plaisirs de vieillard,
Pour quelques jours de plus dont Dieu seul sait le compte,
Ton père sous ses pieds, te marchandait ta honte,
Et cet affreux tréteau, chose horrible à penser !
Qu'un matin le bourreau vint en Grève dresser,
Avant la fin du jour devait être, ô misère !
Ou le lit de la fille, ou l'échafaud du père !
O Dieu ! qui nous jugez, qu'avez-vous dit là-haut,
Quand vos regards ont vu, sur ce même échafaud,
Se vautrer, triste et louche, et sanglante et souillée,
La luxure royale en clémence habillée ?
Sire ! en faisant cela, vous avez mal agi.
Que du sang d'un vieillard le pavé fût rougi,
C'était bien.   Ce vieillard, peut-être respectable,
Le méritait, étant de ceux du connétable.
Mais que pour le vieillard vous ayez pris l'enfant,
Que vous ayez broyé sous un pied triomphant
La pauvre femme en pleurs, à s'effrayer trop prompte,
C'est une chose impie, et dont vous rendrez compte !
Vous avez dépassé votre droit d'un grand pas.
Le père était à vous, mais la fille non pas.

Ah ! vous m'avez fait grâce !—Ah! vous nommez la chose
Une grâce ! et je suis un ingrat, je suppose !
—Sire, au lieu d'abuser ma fille, bien plutôt
Que n'êtes-vous venu vous-même en mon cachot !
Je vous aurais crié :—Faites-moi mourir ! grâce !
Oh ! grâce pour ma fille, et grâce pour ma race !
Oh ! faites-moi mourir ! la tombe, et non l'affront !
Pas de tête plutôt qu'une souillure au front !
Oh ! monseigneur le roi, puisqu'ainsi l'on vous nomme,
Croyez-vous qu'un chrétien, un comte, un gentilhomme,
Soit moins décapité, répondez, monseigneur,
Quand au lieu de la tête il lui manque l'honneur ?
—J'aurais dit cela, sire, et le soir, dans l'église,
Dans mon cercueil sanglant baisant ma barbe grise,
Ma Diane au cœur pur, ma fille au front sacré,
Honorée, eût prié pour son père honoré !
—Sire, je ne viens pas redemander ma fille.
Quand on n'a plus d'honneur, on n'a plus de famille.
Qu'elle vous aime ou non d'un amour insensé,
Je n'ai rien à reprendre où la honte a passé.
Gardez-la.—Seulement je me suis mis en tête
De venir vous troubler ainsi dans chaque fête,
Et jusqu'à ce qu'un père, un frère, ou quelque époux,
—La chose arrivera,—nous ait vengés de vous,
Pâle, à tous vos banquets, je reviendrai vous dire :
—Vous avez mal agi, vous avez mal fait, sire !—
Et vous m'écouterez, et votre front terni
Ne se relèvera que quand j'aurai fini.
Vous voudrez, pour forcer ma vengeance à se taire,
Me rendre au bourreau. Non. Vous ne l'oserez faire,
De peur que ce ne soit mon spectre qui demain
                    (*Montrant sa tête*)
Revienne vous parler,—cette tête à la main !

Marion de Lorme had been prohibited by Charles the
Tenth for an imaginary reflection on Charles the Tenth ;
Le Roi s'amuse was prohibited by Louis-Philippe the First

—and Last—for an imaginary reflection on Citizen Philippe
Égalité. Victor Hugo vindicated his meaning and re-
claimed his rights in a most eloquent, most manly, and
most unanswerable speech before a tribunal which durst
not and could not but refuse him justice. Early in the
following year he brought out the first of his three tragedies
in prose—in a prose which even the most loyal lovers of
poetry, Théophile Gautier at their head, acknowledged on
trial to be as good as verse. And assuredly it would be, if
any prose ever could : which yet I must confess that I for
one can never really feel to be possible. *Lucrèce Borgia*,
the first-born of these three, is also the most perfect in structure as well as the most sublime in subject. The plots of all
three are equally pure inventions of tragic fancy : Gennaro
and Fabiano, the heroic son of the Borgia and the caitiff
lover of the Tudor, are of course as utterly unknown to history as is the self-devotion of the actress Tisbe. It is more
important to remark and more useful to remember that the
mastery of terror and pity, the command of all passions and
all powers that may subserve the purpose of tragedy, is
equally triumphant and infallible in them all. *Lucrèce Borgia* and *Marie Tudor* appeared respectively in February and
in November of the year 1833 ; *Angelo*, two years later ;
and the year after this the exquisite and melodious libretto
of *La Esmeralda*, which should be carefully and lovingly
studied by all who would appreciate the all but superhuman
versatility and dexterity of metrical accomplishment which
would have sufficed to make a lesser poet famous among his
peers for ever, but may almost escape notice in the splendour of Victor Hugo's other and sublimer qualities. In his
thirty-seventh year all these blazed out once more together

in the tragedy sometimes apparently rated as his master-work
by judges whose verdict would on any such question be
worthy at least of all considerate respect. No one that I
know of has ever been absurd enough to make identity in
tone of thought or feeling, in quality of spirit or of style, the
ground for a comparison of Hugo with Shakespeare : they
are of course as widely different as are their respective
countries and their respective times : but never since the
death of Shakespeare had there been so perfect and harmonious a fusion of the highest comedy with the deepest
tragedy as in the five many-voiced and many-coloured acts
of *Ruy Blas.*

At the age of forty Victor Hugo gave to the stage which
for thirteen years had been glorified by his genius the last
work he was ever to write for it. There may perhaps be
other readers besides myself who take even more delight in
Les Burgraves than in some of the preceding plays which
had been more regular in action, more plausible in story,
less open to the magnificent reproach of being too good for
the stage—as the *Hamlet* which came finally from the re-
casting hand of Shakespeare was found to be, in the judgment even of Shakespeare's fellows ; too rich in lyric beauty,
too superb in epic state. The previous year had seen the
publication of the marvellously eloquent, copious, and vivid
letters which gave to the world the impressions received by
its greatest poet in a tour on the Rhine made five years
earlier—that is, in the year of *Ruy Blas.* In this book, as
Gautier at once observed, the inspiration of *Les Burgraves*
is evidently and easily traceable. Among numberless masterpieces of description, from which I have barely time to select
for mention the view of Bishop Hatto's tower by the appro-

priately Dantesque light of a furnace at midnight—not as
better than others, but as an example of the magic by which
the writer imbues and impregnates observation and recollection with feeling and with fancy—the most enchanting legend
of enchantment ever written for children of all ages, sweet
and strange enough to have grown up among the fairy
tales of the past whose only known authors are the winds
and suns of their various climates, lurks like a flower in a
crevice of a crumbling fortress.   The entrancing and haunt-
ing beauty of Régina's words as she watches the departing
swallows—words which it may seem that any one might
have said, but to which none other could have given the
accent and the effect that Hugo has thrown into the simple
sound of them—was as surely derived, we cannot but think,
from some such milder and brighter vision of the remembered Rhineland solitudes, as were the sublime and all but
Æschylean imprecations of Guanhumara from the impression
of their darker and more savage memories or landscapes.

OTBERT (*lui montrant la fenêtre*).
Voyez ce beau soleil !

RÉGINA.
Oui, le couchant s'enflamme.
Nous sommes en automne et nous sommes au soir.
Partout la feuille tombe et le bois devient noir.

OTBERT.
Les feuilles renaîtront.

RÉGINA.
Oui.
(*Rêvant et regardant le ciel*)
Vite ! à tire-d'ailes !—
—Oh ! c'est triste de voir s'enfuir les hirondelles !—
Elles s'en vont là-bas, vers le midi doré.

OTBERT.

Elles reviendront.

RÉGINA.

Oui.—Mais moi je ne verrai
Ni l'oiseau revenir ni la feuille renaître !

Two years before the appearance of *Les Burgraves*
Victor Hugo had begun his long and glorious career as an
orator by a speech of characteristically generous enthusiasm,
delivered on his reception into the Academy. The forgotten
playwright and versifier whom he succeeded had been a
professional if not a personal enemy : the one memorable
thing about the man was his high-minded opposition to the
tyranny of Napoleon, his own personal friend before the
epoch of that tyranny began : and this was the point at once
seized and dwelt on by the orator in a tone of earnest and
cordial respect. The fiery and rapturous eloquence with
which at the same time he celebrated the martial triumphs
of the empire gave ample proof that he was now, as his
father had prophesied that his mother's royalist boy would
become when he grew to be a man, a convert to the views
of that father, a distinguished though ill-requited soldier of
the empire, and a faithful champion or mourner of its cause.
The stage of Napoleonic hero-worship, single-minded and
single-eyed if short-sighted and misdirected, through which
Victor Hugo was still passing on towards the unseen prospect
of a better faith, had been vividly illustrated and vehemently
proclaimed in his letters on the Rhine, and was hereafter to
be described with a fervent and pathetic fidelity in a famous
chapter of *Les Misérables*. The same phase of patriotic
prepossession inspired his no less generous tribute to the

not very radiant memory of Casimir Delavigne, to whom he paid likewise the last and crowning honour of a funeral oration : an honour afterwards conferred on Frédéric Soulié, and far more deservedly bestowed on Honoré de Balzac. More generous his first political speech in the chamber of peers could not be, but there was more of reason and justice in its fruitless appeal for more than barren sympathy, for a moral though not material intervention, on behalf of Poland in 1846. His second speech as a peer is an edifying commentary on the vulgar English view of his character as defective in all the practical and rational qualities of a politician, a statesman, or a patriot. The subject was the consolidation and defence of the French coast-line : a poet, of course, according to all reasonable tradition, if he ventured to open his unserviceable lips at all on such a grave matter of public business, ought to have remembered what was expected of him by the sagacity of blockheads, and carefully confined himself to the clouds, leaving facts to take care of themselves and proofs to hang floating in the air, while his vague and verbose declamation wandered at its own sweet will about and about the matter in hand, and never came close enough to grapple it. This, I regret to say, is exactly what the greatest poet of his age was inconsiderate enough to avoid, and most markedly to abstain from doing ; a course of conduct which can only be attributed to his notorious and deplorable love of paradox. His speech, though not wanting in eloquence of a reserved and masculine order, was wholly occupied with sedate and business-like exposition of facts and suggestion of remedies, grounded on experience and study of the question, and resulting in a proposal at once scientific and direct for such research as might result if possible in an arrest of the double danger with which the coast was threatened by the advance of the Atlantic and the Channel to a gradual obstruction of the great harbours and by the withdrawal or subsidence of the Mediterranean from the sea-ports of the south ; finally, the orator urged upon his audience as a crowning necessity the creation of fresh harbours of refuge in dangerous and neglected parts of the coast ; insisting, with a simple and serious energy somewhat unlike the imaginary tone of the typical or traditional poet, on the plain fact that ninety-two ships had been lost on the same part of the coast within a space of seven years, which might have been saved by the existence of a harbour of refuge. To an Olympian or a Nephelococcygian intelligence such a paltry matter should have been even more indifferent than the claim of a family of exiles on the compassion of the country which had expelled them. To my own more humble and homely understanding it seems that there are not many more significant or memorable facts on record in the history of our age than this : that Victor Hugo was the advocate whose pleading brought back to France the banished race of which the future representative was for upwards of twenty years to keep him in banishment from France. On the evening of the same day on which the house of peers had listened to his speech in behalf of the Bonaparte family, Louis-Philippe, having taken cognizance of it, expressed his intention to authorize the return of the brood whose chief was hereafter to pick the pockets of his children. In the first fortnight of the following year the future author of the terrible *Vision of Dante* saluted in words full of noble and fervent reverence the apostle of Italian resur-

rection and Italian unity in the radiant figure of Pope Pius
the Ninth. When the next month's revolution had flung
Louis-Philippe from his throne, Victor Hugo declined to
offer himself to the electors as a candidate for a seat in the
assembly about to undertake the charge of framing a consti-
tution for the commonwealth ; but, if summoned by his
fellow-citizens to take his share of this task, he expressed
himself ready to discharge the duty so imposed on him with
the disinterested self-devotion of which his whole future
career was to give such continuous and such austere evidence. From the day on which sixty thousand voices summoned him to redeem this pledge, he never stinted nor
slackened his efforts to fulfil the charge he had accepted in
the closing words of a short, simple, and earnest address, in
which he placed before his electors the contrasted likenesses
of two different republics ; one, misnamed a commonweal,
the rule of the red flag, of barbarism and blindness, com-
munism and proscription and revenge ; the other a commonwealth indeed, in which all rights should be respected
and no duties evaded or ignored ; a government of justice
and mercy, of practicable principles and equitable freedom,
of no iniquitous traditions and no utopian aims. To establish this kind of commonwealth and prevent the resurrection of the other, Hugo, at the age of forty-six, professed
himself ready to devote his life. The work of thirty-seven
years is now before all men's eyes for proof how well this
promise has been kept. On dangerous questions of perverse
or perverted socialism (June 20, 1848), on the freedom of
the press, on the state of siege, its temporary necessity and
its imminent abuse, on the encouragement of letters and
the freedom of the stage, he spoke, in the course of a few

months, with what seems to my poor understanding the
most admirable good sense and temperance, the most perfect moderation and loyalty   I venture to dwell upon this
division of Hugo's life and labours with as little wish of
converting as I could have hope to convert that large
majority whose verdict has established as a law of nature the
fact or the doctrine that ' every poet is a fool ' when he
meddles with practical politics ; but not without a confidence grounded on no superficial study that the maintainers
of this opinion, if they wish to cite in support of it the evidence supplied by Victor Hugo's political career, will do
well to persevere in the course which I will do them the
justice to admit that—as far as I know—they have always
hitherto adopted ; in other words, to assume the universal
assent of all persons worth mentioning to the accuracy of
this previous assumption, and dismiss with a quiet smile or
an open sneer the impossible notion that any one but some
single imbecile or eccentric can pretend to take seriously
what seems to them ridiculous, or to think that ridiculous
which to their wiser minds commends itself as serious.
This beaten road of assumption, this well-worn highway of
assertion, is a safe as well as a simple line of travel : and the
practical person who keeps to it can well afford to dispense
with argument as palpably superfluous, and with evidence as
obviously impertinent.   Should he so far forget that great
principle of precaution as to diverge from it into the modest
and simple course of investigation and comparison of theory
with fact and probability with proof, his task may be somewhat harder, and its result somewhat less than satisfactory.
I would not advise any but an honest and candid believer
in the theory which identifies genius with idiocy—which at

all events would practically define one special form of genius
as a note of general idiocy—to study the speeches (they are
nine in number, including two brief and final replies to the
personal attacks of one Montalembert, whose name used to
be rather popular among a certain class of English journalists
as that of a practical worshipper of their great god Compro-
mise, and a professional enemy of all tyranny or villainy that
was not serviceable and obsequious to his Church)—to study,
I say, the speeches delivered by Victor Hugo in the Legisla
tive Assembly during a space of exactly two years and eight
days.   The first of these speeches dealt with the question
of what in England we call pauperism—with the possibility,
the necessity, and the duty of its immediate relief and its
ultimate removal : the second, with the infamous and inex-
piable crime which diverted against the Roman republic an
expedition sent out under the plea of protecting Rome
against the atrocities of Austrian triumph.   A double-faced
and double-dealing law, which under the name or the mask
of free education aimed at securing for clerical instruction a
monopoly of public support and national encouragement,
was exposed and denounced by Hugo in a speech which
insisted no less earnestly and eloquently on the spiritual duty
and the spiritual necessity of faith and hope than on the
practical necessity and duty of vigilant resistance to priestly
pretention, and vigilant exposure of ecclesiastical hypocrisy
and reactionary intrigue.   Against ' the dry guillotine ' of
imprisonment in a tropical climate added to transportation
for political offences, the whole eloquence of a heart as great
as his genius was poured forth in fervour of indignation and
pity, of passion and reason   combined.   The next trick of
the infamous game played by the conspirators against the

commonwealth, who were now beginning to show their hand, was the mutilation of the suffrage. To this again Victor Hugo opposed the same steadfast front of earnest and rational resistance ; and yet again to the sidelong attack of the same political gang on the existing freedom of the press. A year and eight days elapsed before the delivery of his next and last great speech in the Assembly which he would fain have saved from the shame and ruin then hard at hand—the harvest of its own unprincipled infatuation. The fruit of conspiracy, long manured with fraud and falsehood and all the furtive impurities of intrigue, was now ripe even to rottenness, and ready to fall into the hands already stretched towards it—into the lips yet open to protest that no one—the accuser himself must know it—that no one was dreaming of a second French empire. All that reason and indignation, eloquence and argument, loyalty and sincerity could do to save the commonwealth from destruction and the country from disgrace, was done : how utterly in vain is matter of history—of one among the darkest pages in the roll of its criminal records. The voice of truth and honour was roared and hooted down by the faction whose tactics would have discredited a den of less dishonest and more barefaced thieves ; the stroke of state was ready for striking ; and the orator's next address was the utterance of an exile.

There are not, even in the whole work of Victor Hugo, many pages of deeper and more pathetic interest than those which explain to us 'what exile is.' Each of the three prefaces to the three volumes of his *Actes et Paroles* is rich in living eloquence, in splendid epigram and description, narrative and satire and study of men and things : but the second, it seems to me, would still be first in attraction, if it had no other claim than this, that it contains the record of the death of Captain Harvey. No reverence for innocent and heroic suffering, no abhorrence of triumphant and execrable crime, can impede or interfere with our sense of the incalculable profit, the measureless addition to his glory and our gain, resulting from Victor Hugo's exile of nineteen years and nine months. Greater already than all other poets of his time together, these years were to make him greater than any but the very greatest of all time. His first task was of course the discharge of a direct and practical duty ; the record or registration of the events he had just witnessed, the infliction on the principal agent in them of the simple and immediate chastisement consisting in the delineation of his character and the recapitulation of his work. There would seem to be among modern Englishmen an impression—somewhat singular, it appears to me, in a race which professes to hold in special reverence a book so dependent for its arguments and its effects on a continuous appeal to conscience and emotion as the Bible—that the presence of passion, be it never so righteous, so rational, so inevitable by any one not ignoble or insane, implies the absence of reason ; that such indignation as inflamed the lips of Elijah with prophecy, and armed the hand of Jesus with a scourge, is a sign— except of course in Palestine of old—that the person affected by this kind of moral excitement must needs be a lunatic of the sentimental if not rather of the criminal type. The main facts recorded in the pages of *Napoléon le Petit* and *L'Histoire d'un Crime* are simple, flagrant, palpable, indisputable. The man who takes any other view of them than is expressed in these two books must be prepared to impugn and to confute the principle that perjury, robbery, and

murder are crimes.   But, we are told, the perpetual vehe-
mence of incessant imprecation, the stormy insistence of un-
remitting obloquy, which accompanies every chapter, illu-
minates every page, underlines every sentence of the narrative, must needs impair the confidence of an impartial reader
in the trustworthiness of a chronicle and a commentary
written throughout as in characters of flaming fire.   Englishmen are proud to prefer a more temperate, a more practical,
a more sedate form of political or controversial eloquence.
When I remember and consider certain examples of popular
oratory and controversy now flagrant and flourishing among
us, I am tempted to doubt the exact accuracy of this un-
doubtedly plausible proposition: but, be that as it may, I must
take leave to doubt yet more emphatically the implied conclusion that the best or the only good witness procurable on a
question of right and wrong is one too impartial to feel enthusiasm or indignation; that indifference alike to good and evil
is the sign of perfect equity and trustworthiness in a judge of
moral or political questions; that a man who has witnessed
a deliberate massacre of unarmed men, women, and children,
if he be indiscreet enough to describe his experience in any
tone but that of a scientific or æsthetic serenity, forfeits the
inherent right of a reasonable and an honourable man to
command a respectful and attentive hearing from all honourable and reasonable men.

   But, valuable and precious as all such readers will always
hold these two books of immediate and implacable history,
they will not, I presume, be rated among the more important
labours of their author's literary life.   No one who would
know fully or would estimate aright the greatest genius born
into the world in our nineteenth century can afford to pass

them by with less than careful and sympathetic study : for without moral sympathy no care will enable a student to form any but a trivial and a frivolous judgment on writings which make their primary appeal to the conscience—to the moral instinct and the moral intelligence of the reader.   They may perhaps not improperly be classed, for historic or biographic interest, with the *Littérature et Philosophie mêlées* which had been given to the world in 1834.   From the crudest impressions of the boy to the ripest convictions of the man, one common quality informs and harmonizes every stage of thought, every phase of feeling, every change of spiritual outlook, which has left its mark on the writings of which that collection is composed ; the quality of a pure, a perfect, an intense and burning sincerity.   Apart from this personal interest which informs them all, two at least are indispensable to any serious and thorough study of Hugo's work : the fervent and reiterated intercession on behalf of the worse than neglected treasures of mediæval architecture then delivered over for a prey to the claws of the destroyer and the paws of the restorer ; the superb essay on Mirabeau, which remains as a landmark or a tidemark in the history of his opinions and the development of his powers.   But the highest expression of these was not to be given in prose—not even in the prose of Victor Hugo.

There is not, it seems to me, in all this marvellous life, to which wellnigh every year brought its additional aureole of glory, a point more important, a date more memorable, than the publication of the *Châtiments*.   Between the prologue *Night* and the epilogue *Light* the ninety-eight poems that roll and break and lighten and thunder like waves of a visible sea fulfil the choir of their crescent and refluent

harmonies with hardly less depth and change and strength
of music, with no less living force and with no less passionate
unity, than the waters on whose shores they were written.
Two poems, the third and the sixth, in the first of the seven
books into which the collection is divided, may be taken as
immediate and sufficient instances of the two different keys
in which the entire book is written ; of the two styles, one
bitterly and keenly realistic, keeping scornfully close to
shameful fact—one higher in flight and wider in range of
outlook, soaring strongly to the very summits of lyric passion—which alternate in terrible and sublime antiphony
throughout the living pages of this imperishable record. A
second Juvenal might have drawn for us with not less of
angry fidelity and superb disgust the ludicrous and loathsome inmates of the den infested by holy hirelings of the
clerical press : no Roman satirist could have sung, no Roman
lyrist could have thundered, such a poem as that which has
blasted for ever the name and the memory of the prostitute
archbishop Sibour. The poniard of the priest who struck
him dead at the altar he had desecrated struck a blow less
deep and deadly than had been dealt already on the rene-
gade pander of a far more infamous assassin. The next
poem is a notable and remarkable example of the fusion
sometimes accomplished—or, if this be thought a phrase
too strong for accuracy, of the middle note sometimes
touched, of the middle way sometimes taken—between the
purely lyric and the purely satiric style or method. But it
would be necessary to dwell on every poem, to pause at
every page, if adequate justice were to be done to this or
indeed to any of the volumes of verse published from this
time forth by Victor Hugo. I will therefore, not without

serious diffidence, venture once more to indicate by selection such poems as seem to me most especially notable
among the greatest even of these.   In the first book, besides
the three already mentioned, I take for examples the solemn
utterance of indignant mourning addressed to the murdered
dead of the fourth of December ; the ringing song in praise
of art which ends in a note of noble menace ; the scornful
song that follows it, with a burden so majestic in its variations ; the fearful and faithful ' map of Europe ' in 1852,
with its closing word of witness for prophetic hope and faith ;
and the simple perfection of pathos in the song of the little
forsaken birds and lambs and children.   In the second book,
the appeal ' To the People,' with a threefold cry for burden,
calling on the buried Lazarus to rise again in words that
seem to reverberate from stanza to stanza like peal upon
peal of living thunder, prolonged in steadfast cadence from
height to height across the hollows of a range of mountains,
is one of the most wonderful symphonies of tragic and
triumphant verse that ever shook the hearts of its hearers
with rapture of rage and pity.   The first and the two last
stanzas seem to me absolutely unsurpassed and unsurpassable for pathetic majesty of music.

> Partout pleurs, sanglots, cris funèbres.
> Pourquoi dors-tu dans les ténèbres ?
> Je ne veux pas que tu sois mort.
> Pourquoi dors-tu dans les ténèbres ?
> Ce n'est pas l'instant où l'on dort.
> La pâle Liberté gît sanglante à ta porte.
> Tu le sais, toi mort, elle est morte.
> Voici le chacal sur ton seuil,
> Voici les rats et les belettes,
> Pourquoi t'es-tu laissé lier de bandelettes ?

Ils te mordent dans ton cerceuil !
De tous les peuples on prépare
    Le convoi . . .—
Lazare ! Lazare ! Lazare !
    Lève-toi !

  .   .   .   .   .

Ils bâtissent des prisons neuves ;
O dormeur sombre, entends les fleuves
Murmurer, teints de sang vermeil ;
Entends pleurer les pauvres veuves,
O noir dormeur au dur sommeil !
Martyrs, adieu ! le vent souffle, les pontons flottent,
Les mères au front gris sanglotent ;
Leurs fils sont en proie aux vainqueurs ;
Elles gémissent sur la route ;
Les pleurs qui de leurs yeux s'échappent goutte à goutte
Filtrent en haine dans nos cœurs.
Les juifs triomphent, groupe avare
    Et sans foi . . .—
Lazare ! Lazare ! Lazare !
    Lève-toi !

Mais, il semble qu'on se réveille !
Est-ce toi que j'ai dans l'oreille,
Bourdonnement du sombre essaim ?
Dans la ruche frémit l'abeille ;
J'entends sourdre un vague tocsin.
Les césars, oubliant qu'il est des gémonies,
S'endorment dans les symphonies,
Du lac Baltique au mont Etna ;
Les peuples sont dans la nuit noire ;
Dormez, rois ; le clairon dit aux tyrans : victoire !
Et l'orgue leur chante : hosanna !
Qui répond à cette fanfare ?
    Le beffroi . . .—
Lazare ! Lazare ! Lazare !
    Lève-toi !

If ever a more superb structure of lyric verse was devised by the brain of man, it must have been, I am very certain, in a language utterly unknown to me. Every line, every pause, every note of it should be studied and restudied by those who would thoroughly understand the lyrical capacity of Hugo's at its very highest point of power, in the fullest sweetness of its strength.

About the next poem—' Souvenir de la nuit du 4 '— others may try, if they please, to write, if they can ; I can only confess that I cannot. Nothing so intolerable in its pathos, I should think, was ever written.

The stately melody of the stanzas in which the exile salutes in a tone of severe content the sorrows that environ and the comforts that sustain him, the island of his refuge, the sea-birds and the sea-rocks and the sea, closes aptly with yet another thought of the mothers weeping for their children.

> Puisque le juste est dans l'abîme,
> Puisqu'on donne le sceptre au crime,
> Puisque tous les droits sont trahis,
> Puisque les plus fiers restent mornes,
> Puisqu'on affiche au coin des bornes
> Le déshonneur de mon pays ;
>
> O République de nos pères,
> Grand Panthéon plein de lumières,
> Dôme d'or dans le libre azur,
> Temple des ombres immortelles,
> Puisqu'on vient avec des échelles
> Coller l'empire sur ton mur ;
>
> Puisque toute âme est affaiblie ;
> Puisqu'on rampe ; puisqu'on oublie
> Le vrai, le pur, le grand, le beau,

Les yeux indignés de l'histoire,
L'honneur, la loi, le droit, la gloire,
Et ceux qui sont dans le tombeau ;

Je t'aime, exil ! douleur, je t'aime !
Tristesse, sois mon diadème.
Je t'aime, altière pauvreté !
J'aime ma porte aux vents battue.
J'aime le deuil, grave statue
Qui vient s'asseoir à mon côté.

J'aime le malheur qui m'éprouve,
Et cette ombre où je vous retrouve,
O vous à qui mon cœur sourit,
Dignité, foi, vertu voilée,
Toi, liberté, fière exilée,
Et toi, dévoûment, grand proscrit !

J'aime cette île solitaire,
Jersey, que la libre Angleterre
Couvre de son vieux pavillon,
L'eau noire, par moments accrue,
Le navire, errante charrue,
Le flot, mystérieux sillon.

J'aime ta mouette, ô mer profonde,
Qui secoue en perles ton onde
Sur son aile aux fauves couleurs,
Plonge dans les lames géantes,
Et sort de ces gueules béantes
Comme l'âme sort des douleurs.

J'aime la roche solennelle
D'où j'entends la plainte éternelle,
Sans trêve comme le remords,
Toujours renaissant dans les ombres,
Des vagues sur les écueils sombres,
Des meres sur leurs enfants morts.

The close of the fourth poem in the third book is a

nobler protest than ever has been uttered or ever can be
uttered in prose against the servile sophism of a false demo-
cracy which affirms or allows that a people has the divine
right of voting itself into bondage.   There is nothing grander
in Juvenal, and nothing more true.

> Ce droit, sachez-le bien, chiens du berger Maupas,
> Et la France et le peuple eux-mêmes ne l'ont pas.
> L'altière Vérité jamais ne tombe en cendre.
> La Liberté n'est pas une guenille à vendre,
> Jetée au tas, pendue au clou chez un fripier.
> Quand un peuple se laisse au piége estropier,
> Le droit sacré, toujours à soi-même fidèle,
> Dans chaque citoyen trouve une citadelle ;
> On s'illustre en bravant un lâche conquérant,
> Et le moindre du peuple en devient le plus grand.
> Donc, trouvez du bonheur, ô plates créatures,
> A vivre dans la fange et dans les pourritures,
> Adorez ce fumier sous ce dais de brocart,
> L'honnête homme recule et s'accoude à l'écart.
> Dans la chute d'autrui je ne veux pas descendre.
> L'honneur n'abdique point.   Nul n'a droit de me prendre
> Ma liberté, mon bien, mon ciel bleu, mon amour.
> Tout l'univers aveugle est sans droit sur le jour.
> Fût-on cent millions d'esclaves, je suis libre.
> Ainsi parle Caton.   Sur la Seine ou le Tibre,
> Personne n'est tombé tant qu'un seul est debout.
> Le vieux sang des aïeux qui s'indigne et qui bout,
> La vertu, la fierté, la justice, l'histoire,
> Toute une nation avec toute sa gloire
> Vit dans le dernier front qui ne veut pas plier.
> Pour soutenir le temple il suffit d'un pilier ;
> Un Français, c'est la France ; un Romain contient Rome,
> Et ce qui brise un peuple avorte aux pieds d'un homme.

The sixth and seventh poems in this book are each a
superb example of its kind ; the verses on an interview

between Abd-el-Kader and Bonaparte are worthy of a place among the earlier *Orientales* for simplicity and fullness of effect in lyric tone and colour ; and satire could hardly give a finer and completer little study than that of the worthy tradesman who for love of his own strong-box would give his vote for a very Phalaris to reign over him, and put up with the brazen bull for love of the golden calf : an epigram which sums up an epoch. The indignant poem of *Joyeuse Vie*, with its terrible photographs of subterranean toil and want, is answered by the not less terrible though ringing and radiant song of *L'empereur s'amuse* ; and this again by the four solemn stanzas in which a whole world of desolate suffering is condensed and realized. The verses of good counsel in which the imperial Macaire is admonished not to take himself too seriously, or trust in the duration of his fair and foul good fortune, are unsurpassed for concentration of contempt. The dialogue of the tyrannicide by the starlit sea with all visible and invisible things that impel or implore him to do justice is so splendid and thrilling in its keen and ardent brevity that we can hardly feel as though a sufficient answer were given to the instinctive reasoning which finds inarticulate utterance in the cry of the human conscience for retribution by a human hand, even when we read the two poems, at once composed and passionate in their austerity, which bid men leave God to deal with the supreme criminal of humanity. *A Night's Lodging*, the last poem of the fourth book, is perhaps the very finest and most perfect example of imaginative and tragic satire that exists : if this rank be due to a poem at once the most vivid in presentation, the most sublime in scorn, the most intense and absolute in condensed expression of abhorrence and in assured expression of belief.

But in the fifth of these seven caskets of chiselled gold and tempered steel there is a pearl of greater price than in any of the four yet opened. The song dated from sea, which takes farewell of all good things and all gladness left behind—of house and home, of the flowers and the sky, of the betrothed bride with her maiden brow—the song which has in its burden the heavy plashing sound of the wave following on the wave that swells and breaks against the bulwarks—the song of darkening waters and darkened lives has in it a magic, for my own ear at least, incomparable in the whole wide world of human song. Even to the greatest poets of all time such a godsend as this—such a breath of instant inspiration—can come but rarely and seem given as by miracle. 'There is sorrow on the sea,' as the prophet said of old ; but when was there sorrow on sea or land which found such piercing and such perfect utterance as this ?

> Adieu, patrie !
> L'onde est en furie.
> Adieu, patrie,
> Azur !

> Adieu, maison, treille au fruit mûr,
> Adieu, les fleurs d'or du vieux mur !

> Adieu, patrie !
> Ciel, forêt, prairie !
> Adieu, patrie,
> Azur !

> Adieu, patrie !
> L'onde est en furie.
> Adieu, patrie,
> Azur !

Adieu, fiancée au front pur,
Le ciel est noir, le vent est dur.

Adieu, patrie !
Lise, Anna, Marie !
Adieu, patrie,
    Azur !

Adieu, patrie !
L'onde est en furie.
Adieu, patrie,
    Azur !

Notre œil, que voile un deuil futur,
Va du flot sombre au sort obscur.

Adieu, patrie !
Pour toi mon cœur prie.
Adieu, patrie,
    Azur !

The next poem is addressed to a disappointed accomplice of the crime still triumphant and imperial in the eyes of his fellow-scoundrels, who seems to have shown signs of a desire to break away from them and a suspicion that even then the ship of empire was beginning to leak—though in fact it had still seventeen years of more or less radiant rascality to float through before it foundered in the ineffable ignominy of Sedan. Full of ringing and stinging eloquence, of keen and sonorous lines or lashes of accumulating scorn, this poem is especially noteworthy for its tribute to the murdered republic of Rome. Certain passages in certain earlier works of Hugo, in *Cromwell* for instance and in *Marie Tudor*, had given rise to a natural and indeed inevitable suspicion of some prejudice or even antipathy on the writer's part which had not less unavoidably aroused a feeling among

Italians that his disposition or tone of mind was anything but cordial or indeed amicable towards their country : a suspicion probably heightened, and a feeling probably sharpened, by his choice of such dramatic subjects from Italian history or tradition as the domestic eccentricities of the exceptional family of Borgia, and the inquisitorial misdirection of the degenerate commonwealth of Venice. To the sense that Hugo was hardly less than an enemy and that Byron had been something more than a well-wisher to Italy I have always attributed the unquestionable and otherwise inexplicable fact that Mazzini should have preferred the pinchbeck and tinsel of Byron to the gold and ivory of Hugo. But it was impossible that the master poet of the world should not live to make amends, if indeed amends were needed, to the country of Mazzini and of Dante.

If I have hardly time to mention the simple and vivid narrative of the martyrdom of Pauline Roland, I must pause at least to dwell for a moment on so famous and so great a poem as *L'Expiation* ; but not to pronounce, or presume to endeavour to decide, which of its several pictures is the most powerful, which of its epic or lyric variations the most impressive and triumphant in effect. The huge historic pageant of ruin, from Moscow to Waterloo, from Waterloo to St. Helena, with the posthumous interlude of apotheosis which the poet had loudly and proudly celebrated just twelve years earlier in an ode, turned suddenly into the peep-show of a murderous mountebank, the tawdry triumph of buffoons besmeared with innocent blood, is so tremendous in its anticlimax that not the sublimest and most miraculous climax imaginable could make so tragic and sublime an impression so indelible from the mind. The slow agony of the great army under the snow ; its rout and dissolution in the supreme hour of panic ; the slower agony, the more gradual dissolution, of the prisoner with a gaoler's eye intent on him to the last ; who can say which of these three is done into verse with most faultless and sovereign power of hand, most pathetic or terrific force and skill ? And the hideous judicial dishonour of the crowning retribution after death, the parody of his empire and the prostitution of his name, is so much more than tragic by reason of the very farce in it that out of ignominy itself and uttermost degradation the poet has made something more august in moral impression than all pageants of battle or of death.

In the sixth book I can but rapidly remark the peculiar beauty and greatness of the lyric lines in which the sound of steady seas regularly breaking on the rocks at Rozel Tower is rendered with so solemn and severe an echo of majestic strength in sadness ; the verses addressed to the people on its likeness and unlikeness to the sea ; the scornful and fiery appeal to the spirit of Juvenal ; the perfect idyllic picture of spring, with all the fruitless exultation of its blossoms and its birds, made suddenly dark and dissonant by recollection of human crime and shame ; the heavenly hopefulness of comfort in the message of the morning star, conveyed into colours of speech and translated into cadences of sound which no painter or musician could achieve.

> Je m'étais endormi la nuit près de la grève.
> Un vent frais m'éveilla, je sortis de mon rêve.
> J'ouvris les yeux, je vis l'étoile du matin.
> Elle resplendissait au fond du ciel lointain
> Dans une blancheur molle, infinie et charmante.
> Aquilon s'enfuyait emportant la tourmente.

L'astre éclatant changeait la nuée en duvet.
C'était une clarté qui pensait, qui vivait ;
Elle apaisait l'écueil où la vague déferle ;
On croyait voir une âme à travers une perle.
Il faisait nuit encor, l'ombre régnait en vain,
Le ciel s'illuminait d'un sourire divin.
La lueur argentait le haut du mât qui penche ;
Le navire était noir, mais la voile était blanche ;
Des goëlands debout sur un escarpement,
Attentifs, contemplaient l'étoile gravement
Comme un oiseau céleste et fait d'une étincelle ;
L'océan, qui ressemble au peuple, allait vers elle,
Et, rugissant tout bas, la regardait briller,
Et semblait avoir peur de la faire envoler.
Un ineffable amour emplissait l'étendue.
L'herbe verte à mes pieds frissonnait éperdue,
Les oiseaux se parlaient dans les nids ; une fleur
Qui s'éveillait me dit : c'est l'étoile ma sœur.
Et pendant qu'à longs plis l'ombre levait son voile,
J'entendis une voix qui venait de l'étoile
Et qui disait :—Je suis l'astre qui vient d'abord.
Je suis celle qu'on croit dans la tombe et qui sort.
J'ai lui sur le Sina, j'ai lui sur le Taygète ;
Je suis le caillou d'or et de feu que Dieu jette,
Comme avec une fronde, au front noir de la nuit.
Je suis ce qui renaît quand un monde est détruit.
O nations ! je suis la Poésie ardente.
J'ai brillé sur Moïse et j'ai brillé sur Dante.
Le lion océan est amoureux de moi.
J'arrive. Levez-vous, vertu, courage, foi !
Penseurs, esprits ! montez sur la tour, sentinelles !
Paupières, ouvrez-vous ; allumez-vous, prunelles ;
Terre, émeus le sillon ; vie, éveille le bruit ;
Debout, vous qui dormez ; car celui qui me suit,
Car celui qui m'envoie en avant la première,
C'est l'ange Liberté, c'est le géant Lumière !

The first poem of the seventh book, on the falling of the walls of Jericho before the seventh trumpet-blast, is equally great in description and in application ; the third is one of the great lyric masterpieces of all time, the triumphant ballad of the Black Huntsman, unsurpassed in the world for ardour of music and fitful change of note from mystery and terror to rage and tempest and supreme serenity of exultation— 'wind and storm fulfilling his word,' we may literally say of this omnipotent sovereign of song.

The sewer of Rome, a final receptacle for dead dogs and rotting Cæsars, is painted line by line and detail by detail in verse which touches with almost frightful skill the very limit of the possible or permissible to poetry in the way of realistic loathsomeness or photographic horror ; relieved here and there by a rare and exquisite image, a fresh breath or tender touch of loveliness from the open air of the daylight world above. The song on the two Napoleons is a masterpiece of skilful simplicity in contrast of tones and colours. But the song which follows, written to a tune of Beethoven's, has in it something more than the whole soul of music, the whole passion of self-devoted hope and self-transfiguring faith ; it gives the final word of union between sound and spirit, the mutual coronation and consummation of them both.

PATRIA.

Là-haut qui sourit ?
　　Est-ce un esprit ?
　　Est-ce une femme ?
Quel front sombre et doux !
　　Peuple, à genoux !
　　Est-ce notre âme
　　Qui vient à nous ?

Cette figure en deuil
Paraît sur notre seuil,
Et notre antique orgueil
  Sort du cercueil.
Ses fiers regards vainqueurs
Réveillent tous les cœurs,
Les nids dans les buissons,
  Et les chansons.

C'est l'ange du jour ;
  L'espoir, l'amour
  Du cœur qui pense ;
Du monde enchanté
  C'est la clarté.
  Son nom est France
  Ou Vérité.

Bel ange, à ton miroir
Quand s'offre un vil pouvoir,
Tu viens, terrible à voir,
  Sous le ciel noir.
Tu dis au monde : Allons !
Formez vos bataillons !
Et le monde ébloui
  Te répond : Oui.

C'est l'ange de nuit.
  Rois, il vous suit,
  Marquant d'avance
Le fatal moment
  Au firmament.
  Son nom est France
  Ou Châtiment.

Ainsi que nous voyons
En mai les alcyons,
Voguez, ô nations,
  Dans ses rayons !

Son bras aux cieux dressé
Ferme le noir passé
Et les portes de fer
Du sombre enfer.

C'est l'ange de Dieu.
Dans le ciel bleu
Son aile immense
Couvre avec fierté
L'humanité.
Son nom est France
Ou Liberté !

The Caravan, a magnificent picture, is also a magnificent allegory and a magnificent hymn. The poem following sums up in twenty-six lines a whole world of terror and of tempest hurtling and wailing round the wreck of a boat by night. It is followed by a superb appeal against the infliction of death on rascals whose reptile blood would dishonour and defile the scaffold : and this again by an admonition to their chief not to put his trust in the chance of a high place of infamy among the more genuinely imperial hellhounds of historic record. The next poem gives us in perfect and exquisite summary the opinions of a contemporary conservative on a dangerous anarchist of extravagant opinions and disreputable character, whom for example's sake it was at length found necessary to crucify. There is no song more simply and nobly pitiful than that which tells us in its burden how a man may die for lack of his native country as naturally and inevitably as for lack of his daily bread. I cite only the last three stanzas by way of sample.

Les exilés s'en vont pensifs.
Leur âme, hélas ! n'est plus entière.
Ils regardent l'ombre des ifs

Sur les fosses du cimetière ;
L'un songe à l'Allemagne altière,
L'autre au beau pays transalpin,
L'autre à sa Pologne chérie.
—On ne peut pas vivre sans pain ;
On ne peut pas non plus vivre sans la patrie.—

Un proscrit, lassé de souffrir,
Mourait ; calme, il fermait son livre ;
Et je lui dis : ' Pourquoi mourir ? '
Il me répondit : ' Pourquoi vivre ? '
Puis il reprit : ' Je me délivre.
Adieu ! je meurs.   Néron Scapin
Met aux fers la France flétrie. . . .'
—On ne peut pas vivre sans pain ;
On ne peut pas non plus vivre sans la patrie.—

' . . . Je meurs de ne plus voir les champs
Où je regardais l'aube naître,
De ne plus entendre les chants
Que j'entendais de ma fenêtre.
Mon âme est où je ne puis être.
Sous quatre planches de sapin
Enterrez-moi dans la prairie.'
—On ne peut pas vivre sans pain ;
On ne peut pas non plus vivre sans la patrie.

Then, in the later editions of the book, came the great
and terrible poem oh the life and death of the miscreant
marshal who gave the watchword of massacre in the streets
of Paris, and died by the visitation of disease before the
walls of Sebastopol.   There is hardly a more splendid
passage of its kind in all the *Légende des Siècles* than the
description of the departure of the fleet in order of battle
from Constantinople for the Crimea ; nor a loftier passage
of more pathetic austerity in all this book of *Châtiments*

than the final address of the poet to the miserable soul, disembodied at length after long and loathsome suffering, of the murderer and traitor who had earned no soldier's death.[1]

And then come those majestic ' last words ' which will ring for ever in the ears of men till manhood as well as poetry has ceased to have honour among mankind. And then comes a poem so great that I hardly dare venture to attempt a word in its praise. We cannot choose but think, as we read or repeat it, that ' such music was never made ' since the morning stars sang together, and all the sons of God shouted for joy. This epilogue of a book so bitterly and inflexibly tragic begins as with a peal of golden bells, or an outbreak of all April in one choir of sunbright song; proceeds in a graver note of deep and trustful exultation and yearning towards the future ; subsides again into something of a more subdued key, while the poet pleads for his faith in a God of righteousness with the righteous who are ready to despair ; and rises from that tone of awe-stricken and earnest pleading to such a height and rapture of inspiration as no Hebrew psalmist or prophet ever soared beyond in his divinest passion of aspiring trust and worship. It is simply impossible that a human tongue should utter, a human hand should write, anything of more supreme and transcendent beauty than the last ten stanzas of the fourth division of this poem. The passionate and fervent accumu-

---

[1] This poem on Saint-Arnaud is dated from Jersey, and must therefore have been written before the second of November 1855—a date of disgrace for Jersey, if not indeed for England. It appears in the various later editions of the *Châtiments*, but has disappeared from the so-called ' édition définitive.' All readers have a right to ask why—and a right to be answered when they ask.

lation of sublimities, of marvellous images and of infinite
appeal, leaves the sense too dazzled, the soul too entranced
and exalted, to appreciate at first or in full the miraculous
beauty of the language, the superhuman sweetness of the
song.   The reader impervious to such impressions may rest
assured that what he admires in the prophecies or the psalms
of Isaiah or of David is not the inspiration of the text, but
the warrant and sign-manual of the councils and the churches
which command him to admire them on trust.

> Ne possède-t-il pas toute la certitude ?
> Dieu ne remplit-il pas ce monde, notre étude,
>   Du nadir au zénith ?
> Notre sagesse auprès de la sienne est démence ;
> Et n'est-ce pas à lui que la clarté commence,
>   Et que l'ombre finit ?
>
> Ne voit-il pas ramper les hydres sur leurs ventres ?
> Ne regarde-t-il pas jusqu'au fond de leurs antres
>   Atlas et Pélion ?
> Ne connaît-il pas l'heure où la cigogne émigre ?
> Sait-il pas ton entrée et ta sortie, ô tigre,
>   Et ton antre, ô lion ?
>
> Hirondelle, réponds, aigle à l'aile sonore,
> Parle, avez-vous des nids que l'Éternel ignore ?
>   O cerf, quand l'as-tu fui ?
> Renard, ne vois-tu pas ses yeux dans la broussaille ?
> Loup, quand tu sens la nuit une herbe qui tressaille,
>   Ne dis-tu pas : C'est lui !
>
> Puisqu'il sait tout cela, puisqu'il peut toute chose,
> Que ses doigts font jaillir les effets de la cause
>   Comme un noyau d'un fruit,
> Puisqu'il peut mettre un ver dans les pommes de l'arbre,
> Et faire disperser les colonnes de marbre
>   Par le vent de la nuit ;

Puisqu'il bat l'océan pareil au bœuf qui beugle,
Puisqu'il est le voyant et que l'homme est l'aveugle,
      Puisqu'il est le milieu,
Puisque son bras nous porte, et puisqu'à son passage
La comète frissonne ainsi qu'en une cage
      Tremble une étoupe en feu ;

Puisque l'obscure nuit le connaît, puisque l'ombre
Le voit, quand il lui plaît, sauver la nef qui sombre,
      Comment douterions-nous,
Nous qui, fermes et purs, fiers dans nos agonies,
Sommes debout devant toutes les tyrannies,
      Pour lui seul, à genoux !

D'ailleurs, pensons. Nos jours sont des jours d'amertume,
Mais, quand nous étendons les bras dans cette brume,
      Nous sentons une main ;
Quand nous marchons, courbés, dans l'ombre du martyre,
Nous entendons quelqu'un derrière nous nous dire :
      C'est ici le chemin.

O proscrits, l'avenir est aux peuples ! Paix, gloire,
Liberté, reviendront sur des chars de victoire
      Aux foudroyants essieux ;
Ce crime qui triomphe est fumée et mensonge ;
Voilà ce que je puis affirmer, moi qui songe
      L'œil fixé sur les cieux !

Les césars sont plus fiers que les vagues marines,
Mais Dieu dit :—Je mettrai ma boucle en leurs narines,
      Et dans leur bouche un mors,
Et je les traînerai, qu'on cède ou bien qu'on lutte,
Eux et leurs histrions et leurs joueurs de flûte,
      Dans l'ombre où sont les morts !

Dieu dit ; et le granit que foulait leur semelle
S'écroule, et les voilà disparus pêle-mêle
      Dans leurs prospérités !
Aquilon ! aquilon ! qui viens battre nos portes,
Oh ! dis-nous, si c'est toi, souffle, qui les emportes,
      Où les as-tu jetés ?

Three years after the *Châtiments* Victor Hugo published the *Contemplations* ; the book of which he said that if the title did not sound somewhat pretentious it might be called ' the memoirs of a soul.' No book had ever in it more infinite and exquisite variety ; no concert ever diversified and united such inexhaustible melodies with such unsurpassable harmonies. The note of fatherhood was never touched more tenderly than in the opening verses of gentle counsel, whose cadence is fresher and softer than the lapse of rippling water or the sense of falling dew : the picture of the poet's two little daughters in the twilight garden might defy all painters to translate it : the spirit, force, and fun of the controversial poems, overflowing at once with good humour, with serious thought, and with kindly indignation, give life and charm to the obsolete questions of wrangling schools and pedants ; and the last of them, on the divine and creative power of speech, is at once profound and sublime enough to grapple easily and thoroughly with so high and deep a subject. The songs of childish loves and boyish fancies are unequalled by any other poet's known to me for their union of purity and gentleness with a touch of dawning ardour and a hint of shy delight : *Lise*, *La Coccinelle*, *Vieille chanson du jeune temps*, are such sweet miracles of simple perfection as we hardly find except in the old songs of unknown great poets who died and left no name. The twenty-first poem, a lyric idyl of but sixteen lines, has something more than the highest qualities of Theocritus ; in colour and in melody it does but equal the Sicilian at his best, but there are two lines at least in it beyond his reach for depth and majesty of beauty. *Childhood* and *Unity*, two poems of twelve and ten lines respectively, are a pair of such flawless jewels as lie now in no living poet's casket. Among the twenty-eight poems of the second book, if I venture to name with special regard the second and the fourth, two songs uniting the subtle tenderness of Shelley's with the frank simplicity of Shakespeare's ; the large and living landscape in a letter dated from Tréport ; the tenth and the thirteenth poems, two of the most perfect love-songs in the world, written (if the phrase be permissible) in a key of serene rapture ; the ' morning's note,' with its vision of the sublime sweetness of life transfigured in a dream ; *Twilight*, with its opening touches of magical and mystic beauty ; above all, the mournful and tender magnificence of the closing poem, with a pathetic significance in the double date appended to the text : I am ready to confess that it is perhaps presumptuous to express a preference even for these over the others. Yet perhaps it may be permissible to select for transcription two of the sweetest and shortest among them.

> Mes vers fuiraient, doux et frêles,
> Vers votre jardin si beau,
> Si mes vers avaient des ailes,
> Des ailes comme l'oiseau.
>
> Ils voleraient, étincelles,
> Vers votre foyer qui rit,
> Si mes vers avaient des ailes,
> Des ailes comme l'esprit.
>
> Près de vous, purs et fidèles,
> Ils accourraient nuit et jour,
> Si mes vers avaient des ailes,
> Des ailes comme l'amour.

Nothing of Shelley's exceeds this for limpid perfection of

melody, renewed in the next lyric with something of a deeper and more fervent note of music.

> Si vous n'avez rien à me dire,
> Pourquoi venir auprès de moi ?
> Pourquoi me faire ce sourire
> Qui tournerait la tête au roi ?
> Si vous n'avez rien à me dire,,
> Pourquoi venir auprès de moi ?
>
> Si vous n'avez rien à m'apprendre,
> Pourquoi me pressez-vous la main ?
> Sur le rêve angélique et tendre,
> Auquel vous songez en chemin,
> Si vous n'avez rien à m'apprendre,
> Pourquoi me pressez-vous la main ?
>
> Si vous voulez que je m'en aille,
> Pourquoi passez-vous par ici ?
> Lorsque je vous vois, je tressaille :
> C'est ma joie et c'est mon souci.
> Si vous voulez que je m'en aille,
> Pourquoi passez-vous par ici ?

In the third book, which brings us up to the great poet's forty-second year, the noble poem called *Melancholia* has in it a foretaste and a promise of all the passionate meditation, all the studious and indefatigable pity, all the forces of wisdom and of mercy which were to find their completer and supreme expression in *Les Misérables*. In *Saturn* we may trace the same note of earnest and thoughtful meditation on the mystery of evil, on the vision so long cherished by mankind of some purgatorial world, the shrine of expiation or the seat of retribution, which in the final volume of the *Légende des Siècles* was touched again with a yet more august effect : the poem there called *Inferi* resumes and expands the tragic thought here first admitted into speech and first clothed round with music.   The four lines written beneath a crucifix may almost be said to sum up the whole soul and spirit of Christian faith or feeling in the brief hour of its early purity, revived in every age again for some rare and beautiful natures—and for these alone.

> Vous qui pleurez, venez à ce Dieu, car il pleure.
> Vous qui souffrez, venez à lui, car il guérit.
> Vous qui tremblez, venez à lui, car il sourit.
> Vous qui passez, venez à lui, car il demeure.

La Statue, with its grim swift glance over the worldwide rottenness of imperial Rome, finds again an echo yet fuller and more sonorous than the note which it repeats in the poem on Roman decadence which forms the eighth division of the revised and completed *Légende des Siècles*.   The two delicately tender poems on the death of a little child are well relieved by the more terrible tenderness of the poem on a mother found dead of want among her four little children.   In this and the next poem, a vivid and ghastly photograph of vicious poverty, we find again the same spirit of observant and vigilant compassion that inspires and informs the great prose epic of suffering which records the redemption of Jean Valjean : and in the next, suggested by the sight (a sorrowful sight always, except perhaps to very small children or adults yet more diminutive in mental or spiritual size) of a caged lion, we recognize the depth of noble pity which moved its author to write *Le Crapaud*—a poem redeemed in all rational men's eyes from the imminent imputation of repulsive realism by the profound and pathetic beauty of the closing lines—and we may recognize also the imaginative and childlike sympathy with the traditional king of beasts which inspired him long after to write *L'Épopée du Lion* for the benefit of his grandchildren. *Insomnie*, a record of the tribute exacted by the spirit from the body, when the impulse to work and to create will not let the weary work-man take his rest, but enforces him, reluctant and recalci-trant, to rise and gird up his loins for labour in the field of imaginative thought, is itself a piece of work well worth the sacrifice even of the happiness of sleep.   The verses on music, suggested by the figure of a flute-playing shepherd on a bas-relief ; the splendid and finished picture of spring, softened rather than shadowed by the quiet thought of death ; the deep and tender fancy of the dead child's return to its mother through the gateway of a second birth ; the grave sweetness and gentle fervour of the verses on the outcast and detested things of the animal and the vegetable world ; and, last, the nobly thoughtful and eloquent poem on the greatness of such little things as the fire on the shepherd's hearth confronting the star at sunset, which may be com-pared with the *Prayer for all men* in the *Feuilles d'Automne* ; these at least demand a rapid word of thankful recognition before we close the first volume of the *Contemplations*.

The fourth book, as most readers will probably remember, contains the poems written in memory of Victor Hugo's daughter, drowned by the accidental capsizing of a pleasure-boat, just six months and seventeen days after her marriage with the young husband who chose rather to share her death than to save himself alone.   These immortal songs of mourning are almost too sacred for critical appreciation of even the most reverent and subdued order.   There are numberless touches in them of such thrilling beauty, so poignant in their simplicity and so piercing in their truth, that silence is perhaps the best or the only commentary on anything so 'rarely sweet and bitter.' One only may perhaps be cited apart from its fellows : the sublime little poem headed *Mors*.

> Je vis cette faucheuse. Elle était dans son champ.
> Elle allait à grands pas moissonnant et fauchant,
> Noir squelette laissant passer le crépuscule.
> Dans l'ombre où l'on dirait que tout tremble et recule,
> L'homme suivait des yeux les lueurs de sa faulx.
> Et les triomphateurs sous les arcs triomphaux
> Tombaient ; elle changeait en désert Babylone,
> Le trône en échafaud et l'échafaud en trône,
> Les roses en fumier, les enfants en oiseaux,
> L'or en cendre, et les yeux des mères en ruisseaux.
> Et les femmes criaient : Rends-nous ce petit être.
> Pour le faire mourir, pourquoi l'avoir fait naître ?
> Ce n'était qu'un sanglot sur terre, en haut, en bas ;
> Des mains aux doigts osseux sortaient des noirs grabats ;
> Un vent froid bruissait dans les linceuls sans nombre ;
> Les peuples éperdus semblaient sous la faulx sombre
> Un troupeau frissonnant qui dans l'ombre s'enfuit :
> Tout était sous ses pieds deuil, épouvante et nuit.
> Derrière elle, le front baigné de douces flammes,
> Un ange souriant portait la gerbe d'âmes.

The fifth book opens most fitly with an address to the noble poet who was the comrade of the author's exile and the brother of his self-devoted son-in-law. Even Hugo never wrote anything of more stately and superb simplicity than this tribute of fatherly love and praise, so well deserved and so royally bestowed. The second poem, addressed to the son of a poet who had the honour to receive the greatest of all his kind as a passing guest in the first days of his long

exile, is as simple and noble as it is gentle and austere.
The third, written in reply to the expostulations of an old
friend and a distant kinsman, is that admirable vindication
of a man's right to grow wiser, and of his duty to speak the
truth as he comes to see it better, which must have imposed
silence and impressed respect on all assailants if respect for
integrity and genius were possible to the imbecile or the vile,
and if silence or abstinence from insult were possible to the
malignant or the fool. The epilogue, appended nine years
later to this high-minded and brilliant poem, is as noble in
imagination, in feeling, and in expression, as the finest page
in the *Châtiments.*

ÉCRIT EN 1855.

J'ajoute un post-scriptum après neuf ans. J'écoute ;
Etes-vous toujours là ? Vous êtes mort sans doute,
Marquis ; mais d'où je suis on peut parler aux morts.
Ah ! votre cercueil s'ouvre :—Où donc es-tu ?—Dehors.
Comme vous.—Es-tu mort ?—Presque. J'habite l'ombre.
Je suis sur un rocher qu'environne l'eau sombre,
Écueil rongé des flots, de ténèbres chargé,
Où s'assied, ruisselant, le blême naufragé.
—Eh bien, me dites-vous, après ?—La solitude
Autour de moi toujours a la même attitude ;
Je ne vois que l'abîme, et la mer, et les cieux,
Et les nuages noirs qui vont silencieux ;
Mon toit, la nuit, frissonne, et l'ouragan le mêle
Aux souffles effrénés de l'onde et de la grêle ;
Quelqu'un semble clouer un crêpe à l'horizon ;
L'insulte bat de loin le seuil de ma maison ;
Le roc croule sous moi dès que mon pied s'y pose ;
Le vent semble avoir peur de m'approcher, et n'ose
Me dire qu'en baissant la voix et qu'à demi
L'adieu mystérieux que me jette un ami.

La rumeur des vivants s'éteint diminuée.
Tout ce que j'ai rêvé s'est envolé, nuée !
Sur mes jours devenus fantômes, pâle et seul,
Je regarde tomber l'infini, ce linceul.—
Et vous dites :—Après ?—Sous un mont qui surplombe,
Près des flots, j'ai marqué la place de ma tombe ;
Ici, le bruit du gouffre est tout ce qu'on entend ;
Tout est horreur et nuit.—Après ?—Je suis content.

The verses addressed to friends whose love and reverence had not forsaken the exile—to Jules Janin, to Alexandre Dumas, above all to Paul Meurice—are models of stately grace in their utterance of serene and sublime resignation, of loyal and affectionate sincerity : but those addressed to the sharers of his exile—to his wife, to his children, to their friend—have yet a deeper spiritual music in the sweet and severe perfection of their solemn cadence. I have but time to name with a word of homage in passing the famous and faultless little poem *Aux Feuillantines*, fragrant with the memory and musical as the laugh of childhood ; the memorial verses recurring here and there, with such infinite and subtle variations on the same deep theme of mourning or of sympathy ; the great brief studies of lonely landscape, imbued with such grave radiance and such noble melancholy, or kindled with the motion and quickened by the music of the sea : but two poems at all events I must select for more especial tribute of more thankful recognition : the sublime and wonderful vision of the angel who was neither life nor death, but love, more strong than either ; and the all but sublimer allegory couched in verse of such majestic resonance, which shows us the star of Venus in heaven above the ruin of her island on earth. The former and shorter of these is as excellent an example as could be chosen of its author's sovereign simplicity of insight and of style.

APPARITION.

Je vis un ange blanc qui passait sur ma tête ;
Son vol éblouissant apaisait la tempête,
Et faisait taire au loin la mer pleine de bruit.
—Qu'est-ce que tu viens faire, ange, dans cette nuit ?
Lui dis-je.   Il répondit :—Je viens prendre ton âme.—
Et j'eus peur, car je vis que c'était une femme ;
Et je lui dis, tremblant et lui tendant les bras :
—Que me restera-t-il ? car tu t'envoleras.—
Il ne répondit pas ; le ciel que l'ombre assiége
S'éteignait. . . .—Si tu prends mon âme, m'écriai-je,
Où l'emporteras-tu ? montre-moi dans quel lieu.
Il se taisait toujours.—O passant du ciel bleu,
Es-tu la mort ? lui dis-je, ou bien es-tu la vie ?—
Et la nuit augmentait sur mon âme ravie,
Et l'ange devint noir, et dit :—Je suis l'amour.
Mais son front sombre était plus charmant que le jour,
Et je voyais, dans l'ombre où brillaient ses prunelles,
Les astres à travers les plumes de ses ailes.

If nothing were left of Hugo but the sixth book of the *Contemplations*, it would yet be indisputable among those who know anything of poetry that he was among the foremost in the front rank of the greatest poets of all time.   Here, did space allow, it would be necessary for criticism with any pretence to adequacy to say something of every poem in turn, to pause for observation of some beauty beyond reach of others at every successive page.   In the first poem a sublime humility finds such expression as should make manifest to the dullest eye not clouded by malevolence and insolent conceit that when this greatest of modern poets asserts in his own person the high prerogative and assumes for his own spirit the high office of humanity, to confront the darkest problem and to challenge the utmost force of intangible and invisible injustice as of visible and tangible iniquity, of all imaginable as of all actual evil, of superhuman indifference as well as of human wrongdoing, it is no merely personal claim that he puts forward no vainly egotistic arrogance that he displays ; but the right of a reasonable conscience and the duty of a righteous faith, common to all men alike in whom intelligence of right and wrong, perception of duty or conception of conscience, can be said to exist at all. If there be any truth in the notion of any difference between evil and good more serious than the conventional and convenient fabrications of doctrine and assumption, then assuredly the meanest of his creatures in whom the perception of this difference was not utterly extinct would have a right to denounce an omnipotent evil-doer as justly amenable to the sentence inflicted by the thunders of his own unrighteous judgment. How profound and intense was the disbelief of Victor Hugo in the rule or in the existence of any such superhuman malefactor could not be better shown than by the almost polemical passion of his prophetic testimony to that need for faith in a central conscience and a central will on which he has insisted again and again as a crowning and indispensable requisite for moral and spiritual life. From the sublime daring, the self-confidence born of self-devotion, which finds lyrical utterance in the majestic verses headed *Ibo*, through the humble and haughty earnestness of remonstrance and appeal—'humble to God, haughty to man'—which pervades the next three poems, the meditative and studious imagination of the poet passes into the fuller light and larger air of thought which imbues and informs with immortal life every line of the great religious poem called *Pleurs dans la nuit.* In this he touches the highest point of poetic meditation, as in the epilogue to the *Châtiments,* written four months earlier, he had touched the highest point of poetic rapture, possible to the most ardent of believers in his faith and the most unapproachable master of his art. Where all is so lofty in its coherence of construction, so perfect in its harmony of composition, it seems presumptuous to indicate any special miracle of inspired workmanship : yet, as Hugo in his various notes on mediæval architecture was wont to select for exceptional attention and peculiar eloquence of praise this or that part or point of some superb and harmonious building, so am I tempted to dwell for a moment on the sublime imagination, the pathetic passion, of the verses which render into music the idea of a terrene and material purgatory, with its dungeons of flint and cells of clay wherein the spirit imprisoned and imbedded may envy the life and covet the suffering of the meanest animal that toils on earth ; and to set beside this wonderful passage that other which even in a poem so thoroughly imbued with hope and faith finds place and voice for expression of the old mysterious and fantastic horror of the grave, more perfect than ever any mediæval painter or sculptor could achieve.

> Le soir vient ; l'horizon s'emplit d'inquiétude ;
> L'herbe tremble et bruit comme une multitude ;
> Le fleuve blanc reluit ;
> Le paysage obscur prend les veines des marbres
> Ces hydres que, le jour, on appelle des arbres,
> Se tordent dans la nuit.

Le mort est seul. Il sent la nuit qui le dévore.
Quand naît le doux matin, tout l'azur de l'aurore,
          Tous ses rayons si beaux,
Tout l'amour des oiseaux et leurs chansons sans nombre,
Vont aux berceaux dorés ; et, la nuit, toute l'ombre
          Aboutit aux tombeaux.

Il entend des soupirs dans les fosses voisines ;
Il sent la chevelure affreuse des racines
          Entrer dans son cercueil ;
Il est l'être vaincu dont s'empare la chose ;
Il sent un doigt obscur, sous sa paupière close,
          Lui retirer son œil.

Il a froid ; car le soir qui mêle à son haleine
Les ténèbres, l'horreur, le spectre et le phalène,
          Glace ces durs grabats ;
Le cadavre, lié de bandelettes blanches,
Grelotte, et dans sa bière entend les quatre planches
          Qui lui parlent tout bas.

L'une dit :—Je fermais ton coffre-fort.—Et l'autre
Dit :—J'ai servi de porte au toit qui fut le nôtre.—
          L'autre dit :—Aux beaux jours,
La table où rit l'ivresse et que le vin encombre,
C'était moi.—L'autre dit :—J'étais le chevet sombre
          Du lit de tes amours.

Among all the poems which follow, some exquisite in
their mystic tenderness as the elegiac stanzas on *Claire* and
the appealing address to a friend unknown (*À celle qui est
voilée*), others possessed with the same faith and wrestling
with the same questions as beset and sustained the writer
of the poem at which we have just rapidly and reverently
glanced, there are three at least which demand at any rate
one passing word of homage.   The solemn song of medita-

tion 'at the window by night' seems to me to render in its
first six lines the aspects and sounds of sea and cloud and
wind and trees and stars with an utterly incomparable magic
of interpretation.

> Les étoiles, points d'or, percent les branches noires ;
> Le flot huileux et lourd décompose ses moires
>   Sur l'océan blêmi ;
> Les nuages ont l'air d'oiseaux prenant la fuite ;
> Par moments le vent parle, et dit des mots sans suite,
>   Comme un homme endormi.

  No poet but one could have written the three stanzas, so
full of infinite sweetness and awe, inscribed 'to the angels
who see us.'

>   —Passant, qu'es-tu ? je te connais.
> Mais, étant spectre, ombre et nuage,
> Tu n'as plus de sexe ni d'âge.
> —Je suis ta mère, et je venais !
>
>   —Et toi dont l'aile hésite et brille,
> Dont l'œil est noyé de douceur,
> Qu'es-tu, passant ?—Je suis ta sœur.
> —Et toi, qu'es-tu ?—Je suis ta fille.
>
>   —Et toi, qu'es-tu, passant ?—Je suis
> Celle à qui tu disais : Je t'aime !
> —Et toi ?—Je suis ton âme même.—
> Oh ! cachez-moi, profondes nuits !

Nor could any other hand have achieved the pathetic
perfection of the verses in which just thirty years since,
twelve years to a day after the loss of his daughter, and fif-
teen years to a day before the return of liberty which made
possible the return of Victor Hugo to France, his claims

to the rest into which he now has entered, and his reasons for desiring the attainment of that rest, found utterance unexcelled for divine and deep simplicity by any utterance of man on earth.

EN FRAPPANT A UNE PORTE.

J'ai perdu mon père et ma mère,
Mon premier-né, bien jeune, hélas !
Et pour moi la nature entière
  Sonne le glas.

Je dormais entre mes deux frères ;
Enfants, nous étions trois oiseaux ;
Hélas ! le sort change en deux bières
  Leurs deux berceaux.

Je t'ai perdue, ô fille chère,
Toi qui remplis, ô mon orgueil,
Tout mon destin de la lumière
  De ton cercueil !

J'ai su monter, j'ai su descendre.
J'ai vu l'aube et l'ombre en mes cieux.
J'ai connu la pourpre, et la cendre
  Qui me va mieux.

J'ai connu les ardeurs profondes,
J'ai connu les sombres amours ;
J'ai vu fuir les ailes, les ondes,
  Les vents, les jours.

J'ai sur ma tête des orfraies ;
J'ai sur tous mes travaux l'affront,
Au pied la poudre, au cœur des plaies,
  L'épine au front.

J'ai des pleurs à mon œil qui pense,
Des trous à ma robe en lambeau ;
Je n'ai rien à la conscience ;
Ouvre, tombeau.

Last comes the magnificent and rapturous hymn of universal redemption from suffering as from sin, the prophetic
vision of evil absorbed by good, and the very worst of spirits
transfigured into the likeness of the very best, in which the
daring and indomitable faith of the seer finds dauntless and
supreme expression in choral harmonies of unlimited and
illimitable hope. The epilogue which dedicates the book
to the daughter whose grave was now forbidden ground to
her father—so long wont to keep there the autumnal anni-
versary of his mourning—is the very crown and flower of
the immortal work which it inscribes, if we may say so,
rather to the presence than to the memory of the dead.

Not till the thirtieth year from the publication of these
two volumes was the inexhaustible labour of the spirit which
inspired them to cease for a moment—and then, among us
at least, for ever. Three years afterwards appeared the first
series of the *Légende des Siècles*, to be followed nineteen
years later by the second, and by the final complementary
volume six years after that : so that between the inception
and the conclusion of the greatest single work accomplished
in the course of our century a quarter of that century had
elapsed—with stranger and more tragic evolution of events
than any poet or any seer could have foretold or foreseen as
possible. Three years again from this memorable date
appeared the great epic and tragic poem of contemporary
life and of eternal humanity which gave us all the slowly
ripened fruit of the studies and emotions, the passions and

the thoughts, the aspiration and the experience, brought
finally to their full and perfect end in *Les Misérables.* As
the key-note of *Notre-Dame de Paris* was doom—the human
doom of suffering to be nobly or ignobly endured—so the
key-note of its author's next romance was redemption by
acceptance of suffering and discharge of duty in absolute and
entire obedience to the utmost exaction of conscience when
it calls for atonement, of love when it calls for sacrifice of
all that makes life more endurable than death. It is obvious
that no account can here be given of a book which if it re-
quired a sentence would require a volume to express the
character of its quality or the variety of its excellence—the
one unique, the latter infinite as the unique and infinite spirit
whose intelligence and whose goodness gave it life.

Two years after *Les Misérables* appeared the magnificent
book of meditations on the mission of art in the world, on
the duty of human thought towards humanity, inscribed by
Victor Hugo with the name of William Shakespeare. To
allow that it throws more light on the greatest genius of our
own century than on the greatest genius of the age of Shakespeare is not to admit that it is not rich in valuable and
noble contemplations or suggestions on the immediate
subject of Shakespeare's work ; witness the admirably
thoughtful and earnest remarks on Macbeth, the admirably
passionate and pathetic reflections on Lear. The splendid
eloquence and the heroic enthusiasm of Victor Hugo never
found more noble and sustained expression than in this
volume—the spontaneous and inevitable expansion of a pro-
jected preface to his son's incomparable translation of Shakespeare. The preface actually prefixed to it is admirable for
concision, for insight, and for grave historic humour. It

appeared a year after the book which (so to speak) had grown out of it ; and in the same year appeared the *Chansons des Rues et des Bois.* The miraculous dexterity of touch, the dazzling mastery of metre, the infinite fertility in variations on the same air of frolic and thoughtful fancy, would not apparently allow the judges of the moment to perceive or to appreciate the higher and deeper qualities displayed in this volume of lyric idyls. The prologue is a superb example of the power peculiar to its author above all other poets ; the power of seizing on some old symbol or image which may have been in poetic use ever since verse dawned upon the brain of man, and informing it again as with life, and transforming it anew as by fire. Among innumerable exercises and excursions of dainty but indefatigable fancy there are one or two touches of a somewhat deeper note than usual which would hardly be misplaced in the gravest and most ambitious works of imaginative genius. The twelve lines (of four syllables each) addressed *A la belle impérieuse* are such, for example, as none but a great poet of passion, a master of imaginative style, could by any stroke of chance or at any cost of toil have written.

> L'amour, panique
> De la raison,
> Se communique
> Par le frisson.
>
> Laissez-moi dire,
> N'accordez rien.
> Si je soupire,
> Chantez, c'est bien.
>
> Si je demeure,
> Triste, à vos pieds,
> Et si je pleure,
> C'est bien, riez.

Un homme semble
Souvent trompeur.
Mais si je tremble,
Belle, ayez peur.

The sound of the songs of a whole woodland seems to ring like audible spring sunshine through the adorable song of love and youth rejoicing among the ruins of an abbey.

Seuls tous deux, ravis, chantants !
Comme on s'aime !
Comme on cueille le printemps
Que Dieu sème !

Quels rires étincelants
Dans ces ombres
Pleines jadis de fronts blancs,
De cœurs sombres !

On est tout frais mariés.
On s'envoie
Les charmants cris variés
De la joie.

Purs ébats mêlés au vent
Qui frissonne !
Gaîtés que le noir couvent
Assaisonne !

On effeuille des jasmins
Sur la pierre
Où l'abbesse joint ses mains
En prière.

Les tombeaux, de croix marqués,
Font partie
De ces jeux, un peu piqués
Par l'ortie.

On se cherche, on se poursuit,
   On sent croître
Ton aube, amour, dans la nuit
   Du vieux cloître.

On s'en va se becquetant,
   On s'adore,
On s'embrasse à chaque instant,
   Puis encore,

Sous les piliers, les arceaux,
   Et les marbres.
C'est l'histoire des oiseaux
   Dans les arbres.

The inexhaustible exuberance of fancies lavished on the study of the natural church, built by the hawthorn and the nettle in the depth of the living wood, with foliage and wind and flowers, leaves the reader not unfit for such reading actually dazzled with delight. In a far different key, the *Souvenir des vieilles guerres* is one of Hugo's most pathetic and characteristic studies of homely and heroic life. The dialogue which follows, between the irony of scepticism and the enthusiasm of reason, on the progressive ascension of mankind, is at once sublime and subdued in the fervent tranquillity of its final tone : and the next poem, on the so-called ' great age ' and its dwarf of a Cæsar with the sun for a periwig, has in it a whole volume of history and of satire condensed into nine stanzas of four lines of five syllables apiece.

LE GRAND SIÈCLE.

Ce siècle a la forme
D'un monstrueux char.
Sa croissance énorme
Sous un nain césar,

Son air de prodige,
Sa gloire qui ment,
Mêlent le vertige
A l'écrasement.

Louvois pour ministre,
Scarron pour griffon,
C'est un chant sinistre
Sur un air bouffon.

Sur sa double roue
Le grand char descend ;
L'une est dans la boue,
L'autre est dans le sang.

La mort au carrosse
Attelle—où va-t-il ?—
Lavrillière atroce,
Roquelaure vil.

Comme un geai dans l'arbre,
Le roi s'y tient fier ;
Son cœur est de marbre,
Son ventre est de chair.

On a pour sa nuque
Et son front vermeil
Fait une perruque
Avec le soleil.

Il règne et végète,
Effrayant zéro
Sur qui se projette
L'ombre du bourreau.

Ce trône est la tombe ;
Et sur le pavé
Quelque chose en tombe
Qu'on n'a point lavé.

The exquisite poem on the closure of the church already described for the winter is as radiant with humour as with tenderness : and the epilogue responds in cadences of august antiphony to the moral and imaginative passion which imbues with life and fire the magnificent music of the prologue.

In the course of the next four years Victor Hugo published the last two great works which were to be dated from the haven of his exile.   It would be the very ineptitude of impertinence for any man's presumption to undertake the classification or registry of his five great romances in positive order of actual merit : but I may perhaps be permitted to say without fear of deserved rèbuke that none is to me personally a treasure of greater price than *Les Travailleurs de la Mer*.   The splendid energy of the book makes the superhuman energy of the hero seem not only possible but natural, and his triumph over all physical impossibilities not only natural but inevitable.   Indeed, when glancing at the animadversions of a certain sort of critics on certain points or passages in this and in the next romance of its author, I am perpetually inclined to address them in the spirit—were it worth while to address them in any wise at all—after the fashion if not after the very phrase of Mirabeau's reply to a less impertinent objector.   Victor Hugo's acquaintance with navigation or other sciences may or may not have been as imperfect as Shakespeare's acquaintance with geography and natural history ; the knowledge of such a man's ignorance or inaccuracy in detail is in either case of exactly equal importance : and the importance of such knowledge is for all men of sense and candour exactly equivalent to zero.

Between the tragedy of Gilliatt and the tragedy of Gwyn-

plaine Victor Hugo published nothing but the glorious
little poem on the slaughter of Mentana, called *La Voix de
Guernesey*, and (in the same year) the eloquent and ardent
effusion of splendid and pensive enthusiasm prefixed to the
manual or guide-book which appeared on the occasion of
the international exhibition at Paris three years before the
collapse of the government which then kept out of France
the Frenchmen most regardful of her honour and their own.
In the year preceding that collapse he published *L'Homme
qui Rit*; a book which those who read it aright have always
ranked and will always rank among his masterpieces. A
year and eight months after the fall of the putative Bonaparte he published the terrible register of *L'Année Terrible*.
More sublime wisdom, more compassionate equity, more
loyal self-devotion, never found expression in verse of more
varied and impassioned and pathetic magnificence. The
memorial poem in which Victor Hugo so royally repaid,
with praise beyond all price couched in verse beyond all
praise, the loyal and constant devotion of Théophile Gautier,
bears the date of All Souls' Day in the autumn of 1872.
For tenderness and nobility of mingling aspiration and recollection, recollection of combatant and triumphant youth,
aspiration towards the serene and sovereign ascension out
of age through death, these majestic lines are worthy not
merely of eternal record, but far more than that—of a distinct and a distinguished place among the poems of Victor
Hugo. They are not to be found in the *édition ne varietur* :
which, I must needs repeat, will have to be altered or
modified by more variations than one before it can be accepted as a sufficient or standard edition of the complete
and final text. In witness of this I cite the closing lines of

a poem now buried in ' the tomb of Théophile Gautier '—
a beautiful volume which has long been out of print.

> Ami, je sens du sort la sombre plénitude ;
> J'ai commencé la mort par de la solitude,
> Je vois mon profond soir vaguement s'étoiler.
> Voici l'heure où je vais, aussi moi, m'en aller.
> Mon fil trop long frissonne et touche presque au glaive ;
> Le vent qui t'emporta doucement me soulève,
> Et je vais suivre ceux qui m'aimaient, moi banni.
> Leur œil fixe m'attire au fond de l'infini.
> J'y cours.   Ne fermez pas la porte funéraire.
>
> Passons, car c'est la loi ; nul ne peut s'y soustraire ;
> Tout penche ; et ce grand siècle avec tous ses rayons
> Entre en cette ombre immense où, pâles, nous fuyons.
> Oh ! quel farouche bruit font dans le crépuscule
> Les chênes qu'on abat pour le bûcher d'Hercule !
> Les chevaux de la Mort se mettent à hennir,
> Et sont joyeux, car l'âge éclatant va finir ;
> Ce siècle altier qui sut dompter le vent contraire
> Expire . . .—O Gautier, toi, leur égal et leur frère,
> Tu pars après Dumas, Lamartine et Musset.
> L'onde antique est tarie où l'on rajeunissait ;
> Comme il n'est plus de Styx il n'est plus de Jouvence.
> Le dur faucheur avec sa large lame avance
> Pensif et pas à pas vers le reste du blé ;
> C'est mon tour ; et la nuit emplit mon œil troublé
> Qui, devinant, hélas, l'avenir des colombes,
> Pleure sur des berceaux et sourit à des tombes.

Two years after the year of terror, the poet who had made
its memory immortal by his record of its changes and its
chances gave to the world his heroic and epic romance of
Quatrevingt-treize ; instinct with all the passion of a deeper
and wider chivalry than that of old, and touched with a

more than Homeric tenderness for motherhood and childhood. This book was written in the space of five months
and twenty-seven days. The next year witnessed only the
collection of the second series of his *Actes et Paroles* (*Pendant l'Exil*), and the publication of two brief and memorable
pamphlets : the one a simple and pathetic record of the two
beloved sons taken from him in such rapid succession, the
other a terse and earnest plea with the judges who had
spared the life of a marshal condemned on a charge of
high treason to spare likewise the life of a private soldier
condemned for a transgression of military discipline. Most
readers will be glad to remember that on this occasion at
least the voice of the intercessor was not uplifted in vain.
A year afterwards he published the third series of *Actes et
Paroles* (*Depuis l'Exil*), with a prefatory essay full of noble
wisdom, of pungent and ardent scorn, of thoughtful and
composed enthusiasm, on the eternal contrast and the everlasting battle between the spirit of clerical Rome and the
spirit of republican Paris.

'Moi qu'un petit enfant rend tout à fait stupide,' I do
not purpose to undertake a review of *L'Art d'être Grand-
père*. It must suffice here to register the fact that the most
absolutely and adorably beautiful book ever written appeared a year after the volume just mentioned, and some
months after the second series of the *Légende des Siècles* ;
that there is not a page in it which is not above all possible
eulogy or thanksgiving ; that nothing was ever conceived
more perfect than such poems—to take but a small handful
for samples—as *Un manque, La sieste, Choses du soir, Ce que
dit le public* (at the Jardin des Plantes or at the Zoological
Gardens ; ages of public ranging from five, which is com-

paratively young, to seven, which is positively old), *Chant sur
le berceau*, the song for a round dance of children, *Le pot cassé,
La mise en liberté, Jeanne endormie*, the delicious *Chanson
de grand-père*, the glorious *Chanson d'ancêtre*, or the third of
the divine and triune poems on the sleep of a little child ;
that after reading these—to say nothing of the rest—it seems
natural to feel as though no other poet had ever known so
fully or enjoyed so wisely or spoken so sweetly and so well
the most precious of truths, the loveliest of loves, the
sweetest and the best of doctrines.

The first of all to see the light appeared in a magazine
which has long ago collapsed under the influence of far
other writers than the greatest of the century.   Every word
of the thirty-eight lines which compose *La Sieste de Jeanne*
—if any speech or memory of man endure so long—will be
treasured as tenderly by generations as remote from the
writer's as now treasure up with thankful wonder and reverence every golden fragment and jewelled spar from the
wreck of Simonides or of Sappho.   It has all the subtle
tenderness which invests the immortal song of Danaë ; and
the union of perfect grace with living passion, as it were
the suffusion of human flesh and blood with heavenly breath
and fire, brings back once again upon our thoughts the name
which is above every name in lyric song.   There is not one
line which could have been written and set where it stands
by the hand of any lesser than the greatest among poets.
For once even the high priest and even the high priestess
of baby-worship who have made their names immortal
among our own by this especial and most gracious attribute
—even William Blake and Christina Rossetti for once are
distanced in the race of song, on their own sweet ground,

across their own peculiar field of Paradise. Not even in the pastures that heard his pipe keep time to the 'Songs of Innocence,' or on the 'wet bird-haunted English lawn' set ringing as from nursery windows at summer sunrise to the faultless joyous music and pealing birdlike laughter of her divine ' Sing-Song,' has there sounded quite such a note as this from the heaven of heavens in which little babies are adored by great poets, the frailest by the most potent of divine and human kind. And above the work in this lovely line of all poets in all time but one, there sits and smiles eternally the adorable baby who helps us for ever to forget all passing perversities of Christianised socialism or bastard Cæsarism which disfigure and diminish the pure proportions and the noble charm of *Aurora Leigh.* Even the most memorable children born to art in Florence, begotten upon stone or canvas by Andrea del Sarto or by Luca della Robbia's very self, must yield to that one the crown of sinless empire and the palm of powerless godhead which attest the natural mystery of their omnipotence ; and which haply may help to explain why no accumulated abominations of cruelty and absurdity which inlay the record of its history and incrust the fabric of its creed can utterly corrode the natal beauty or corrupt the primal charm of a faith which centres at its opening round the worship of a new-born child.

The most accurate and affectionate description that I ever saw or heard given of a baby's incomparable smile, when graciously pleased to permit with courtesy and accept with kindness the votive touch of a reverential finger on its august little cheek, was given long since in the text accompanying a rich and joyous design of childish revel by

Richard Doyle.   A baby in arms is there contemplating the
riotous delights of its elders, fallen indeed from the sovereign state of infancy, but not yet degenerate into the lower
life of adults, with that bland and tacit air of a large-minded
and godlike tolerance which the devout observer will not
fail to have remarked in the aspect of babies when unvexed
and unincensed by any cross accident or any human short-
coming on the part of their attendant ministers.   Possibly a
hand which could paint that inexpressible smile might not
fail also of the ability to render in mere words some sense
of the ineffable quality which rests upon every line and
syllable of this most divine poem.   There are lines in it—
but after all this is but an indirect way of saying that it is
a poem by Victor Hugo—which may be taken as tests of
the uttermost beauty, the extreme perfection, the supreme
capacity and charm, to which the language of men can
attain.   It might seem as if the Fates could not allow
two men capable of such work to live together in one
time of the world ; and that Shelley therefore had to die
in his thirtieth year as soon as Hugo had attained his
twentieth.

> Elle fait au milieu du jour son petit somme ;
> Car l'enfant a besoin du rêve plus que l'homme,
> Cette terre est si laide alors qu'on vient du ciel !
> L'enfant cherche à revoir Chérubin, Ariel,
> Ses camarades, Puck, Titania, les fées,
> Et ses mains quand il dort sont par Dieu réchauffées.
> Oh ! comme nous serions surpris si nous voyions,
> Au fond de ce sommeil sacré, plein de rayons,
> Ces paradis ouverts dans l'ombre, et ces passages
> D'étoiles qui font signe aux enfants d'être sages,
> Ces apparitions, ces éblouissements !
> Donc, à l'heure où les feux du soleil sont calmants,

Quand toute la nature écoute et se recueille,
Vers midi, quand les nids se taisent, quand la feuille
La plus tremblante oublie un instant de frémir,
Jeanne a cette habitude aimable de dormir ;
Et la mère un moment respire et se repose,
Car on se lasse, même à servir une rose.
Ses beaux petits pieds nus dont le pas est peu sûr
Dorment ; et son berceau, qu'entoure un vague azur
Ainsi qu'une auréole entoure une immortelle,
Semble un nuage fait avec de la dentelle ;
On croit, en la voyant dans ce frais berceau-là,
Voir une lueur rose au fond d'un falbala :
On la contemple, on rit, on sent fuir la tristesse,
Et c'est un astre, ayant de plus la petitesse ;
L'ombre, amoureuse d'elle, a l'air de l'adorer ;
Le vent retient son souffle et n'ose respirer.
Soudain, dans l'humble et chaste alcôve maternelle,
Versant tout le matin qu'elle a dans sa prunelle,
Elle ouvre la paupière, étend un bras charmant,
Agite un pied, puis l'autre, et, si divinement
Que des fronts dans l'azur se penchent pour l'entendre,
Elle gazouille . . .—Alors, de sa voix la plus tendre,
Couvant des yeux l'enfant que Dieu fait rayonner,
Cherchant le plus doux nom qu'elle puisse donner
A sa joie, à son ange en fleur, à sa chimère :
—Te voilà réveillée, horreur ! lui dit sa mère.

If the last word on so divine a subject could ever be said, it surely might well be none other than this. But with workmen of the very highest order there is no such thing as a final touch, a point at which they like others are compelled to draw bridle, a summit on which even their genius also may abide but while a man takes breath, and halt without a hope or aspiration to pass beyond it.

Far different in the promise or the menace of its theme, the poet's next work, issued in the following year, was one in spirit with the inner spirit of this book. In sublime simplicity of conception and in sovereign accomplishment of its design, *Le Pape* is excelled by no poem of Hugo's or of man's. In the glory of pure pathos it is perhaps excelled, as in the divine long-suffering of all-merciful wisdom it can be but equalled, by the supreme utterance of *La Pitié Suprême.* In splendour of changeful music and imperial magnificence of illustration the two stand unsurpassed for ever, side by side. A third poem, attacking at once the misbelief or rather the infidelity which studies and rehearses 'the grammar of assent' to creeds and articles of religion, and the blank disbelief or denial which rejects all ideals and all ideas of spiritual life, is not so rich even in satire as in reason, so earnest even in rejection of false doctrine as in assertion of free belief. Upon this book no one can hope to write anything so nearly adequate and so thoroughly worth reading as is the tribute paid to it by Théodore de Banville —the Simonides Melicertes of France.

'In the midst of our confused life, turbulent and flat, bustling and indifferent, where books and plays, dreams and poems, driven down a wind of oblivion, are like the leaves which November sweeps away, and fly past, without giving us time to tell one from another, in a vague whirl and rush, at times there appears a new book by Victor Hugo, and everything lights up, resounds, murmurs, and sings at once.

'The shining, sounding, fascinating verse, with its thousand surprises of tone, of colour, of harmony, breaks forth like a rich concert, and ever newly stirred, dazzled and astonished, as if we were hearing verses for the first time, we remain stupefied with wonder before the persistent prodigy of the great seer, the great thinker, the unheard-of artist, self-transfigured without ceasing, always new and always like himself. It would be impertinent to say of him that he makes progress ; and yet I find

no other word to express the fact that every hour, every minute
he adds something new, something yet more exact and yet more
caressing, to that swing of syllables, that melodious play of
rhyme renascent of itself, which is the grace and the invincible
power of French poetry,'—

if English ears could but learn or would but hear it; whereas
usually they have never been taught even the rudiments of
French prosody, and receive the most perfect cadences of
the most glorious or the most exquisite French poetry as a
schoolboy's who has not yet learnt scansion might receive
the melodies of Catullus or of Virgil.

'Let me be forgiven a seeming blasphemy; but since the
time of periphrasis is over the real truth of things must be said
of them. Well, then, the great peril of poetry is the risk it runs
of becoming a weariness : for it may be almost sublime and yet
perfectly wearisome : but, on the contrary, with all its bewilder-
ing flight, its vast circumference, and the rage of a genius
intoxicated with things immeasurable, the poetry of Victor
Hugo is of itself *amusing* into the bargain—amusing as a fairy
tale, as a many-coloured festival, as a lawless and charming
comedy; for in it words play unexpected parts, take on themselves a special and intense life, put on strange or graceful
faces, clash one against another either cymbals of gold or urns
of crystal, exchange flashes of living light and dawn.

'And let no one suspect in my choice of an epithet any idea
of diminution; a garden-box on the window-sill may be thoroughly wearisome, and an immense forest may be amusing, with
its shades wherein the nightingale sings, its giant trees with the
blue sky showing through them, its mossy shelters where the
silver brooklet hums its tune through the moistened greenery.
Ay,—this is one of its qualities,—the poetry of Hugo can be
read, can be devoured as one devours a new novel, because it is
varied, surprising, full of the unforeseen, clear of commonplaces,
like nature itself; and of such a limpid clearness as to be within
the reach of every creature who can read, even when it

soars to the highest summits of philosophy and idealism. In fact, to be obscure, confused, unintelligible, is not a rare quality nor one difficult to acquire ; and the first fool you may fall in with can easily attain to it. In this magnificent poem which has just appeared—as, for that matter, in all his other poems— what Victor Hugo does is just to dispel and scatter to the winds of heaven those lessons, those fogs, those rubbish-heaps, those clouds of dark bewildered words with which the sham wise men of all ages have overlaid the plain evidence of truth.'

'The words of Mercury are harsh after the songs of Apollo' ; and I, who cannot pretend even to the gift of eloquence proper to the son of Maia, will not presume to add a word of less valuable homage to the choicer tribute of Banville. The three poems last mentioned were respectively published in three successive years : and in the same year with *Religions et Religion* Victor Hugo published a fourth volume, *L'Âne*, in which the questions of human learning and of human training were handled with pathetic ardour and sympathetic irony. It would be superfluous if not insolent to add that the might of hand, the magic of utterance, the sovereign charm of sound and the superb expression of sense, are equal and incomparable in all.

And next year Victor Hugo gave us *Les Quatre Vents de l'Esprit.* In the first division, the book of satire, every page bears witness that the hand which wrote the *Châtiments* had neither lost its strength nor forgotten its cunning ; it is full of keen sense, of wise wrath, of brilliant reason and of merciful equity. The double drama which follows is one of the deepest and sweetest and richest in various effect among the masterpieces of its author. In *Margarita* we breathe again the same fresh air of heroic mountain-ranges and woodlands inviolable, of winds and flowers and all fair

things and thoughts, which blows through all the brighter
and more gracious interludes of the *Légende des Siècles* : the
figures of Gallus, the libertine by philosophy, and Gunich,
the philosopher of profligacy,—the former a true man and
true lover at heart, the latter a cynic and a courtier to the
core—are as fresh in their novelty as the figures of noble
old age and noble young love are fresh in their renewal and
reimpression of types familiar to all hearts since the sunrise
of *Hernani*. The tragedy which follows this little romantic
comedy is but the more penetrative and piercing in its pathos
and its terror for its bitter and burning vein of realism and
of humour. The lyric book is a casket of jewels rich enough
to outweigh the whole wealth of many a poet. After the
smiling song of old times, the stately song of to-day with its
other stars and its other roses, in sight of the shadow where
grows the deathless flower of death, pale and haggard, with
its shadowy perfume : the song of all sweet waking dreams
and visions, and sweetest among them all the vision of a
tyrant loyally slain : the song on hearing a princess sing,
sweeter than all singing and simple as 'the very virtue of
compassion' : the song of evening, and rest from trouble,
and prayer in sorrow, and hope in death : the many-coloured
and sounding song of seaside winter nights : the song of
three nests, the reed-warbler's and the martlet's made with
moss and straw, in the wall or on the water, and love's with
glances and smiles, in the lover's inmost heart : the song of
the watcher by twilight on the cliff, which strikes a note
afterwards repeated and prolonged in the last issue of the
Légende des Siècles, full of mystery and mourning and fear
and faith : the brief deep note of bewildered sorrow that suc-
ceeds it : the great wild vision of death and night, cast into

words which have the very sound of wind and storm and
water, the very shape and likeness of things actually touched
or seen : the soft and sublime song of dawn as it rises on
the thinker deep sunk in meditation on death and on life to
come : the strange dialogue underground, grim and sweet,
between the corpse and the rose-tree : the song of exile in
May, sweet as flowers and bitter as tears : the lofty poem of
suffering which rejects the old Roman refuge of stoic suicide :
the light swift song of a lover's quarrel between the earth and
the sun in wintertime : the unspeakably sweet song of the
daisy that smiles at coming winter, the star that smiles at
coming night, the soul that smiles at coming death : the most
pathetic and heroic song of all, the cry of exile towards the
graves of the beloved over sea, that weeps and is not weary :
the simple and sublime verses on the mountain desolation
to which truth and conscience were the guides : the four
magnificent studies of sea and land, *Promenades dans les
rochers* : the admirable verses on that holy mystery of terror
perceptible in the most glorious works alike of nature and of
poetry : all these and more are fitly wound up by the noble
hymn on planting the oak of the United States of Europe in
the garden of the house of exile.   A few of the briefer among
these may here be taken as examples of a gift not merely
unequalled but unapproached by any but the greatest among
poets.   And first we may choose the following unsurpassable
psalm of evensong.

> Un hymne harmonieux sort des feuilles du tremble ;
> Les voyageurs craintifs, qui vont la nuit ensemble,
> Haussent la voix dans l'ombre où l'on doit se hâter.
> > Laissez tout ce qui tremble
> > > Chanter.

Les marins fatigués sommeillent sur le gouffre.
La mer bleue où Vésuve épand ses flots de soufre
Se tait dès qu'il s'éteint, et cesse de gémir.
    Laissez tout ce qui souffre
      Dormir.

Quand la vie est mauvaise on la rêve meilleure.
Les yeux en pleurs au ciel se lèvent à toute heure ;
L'espoir vers Dieu se tourne et Dieu l'entend crier.
    Laissez tout ce qui pleure
      Prier.

C'est pour renaître ailleurs qu'ici-bas on succombe.
Tout ce qui tourbillonne appartient à la tombe.
Il faut dans le grand tout tôt ou tard s'absorber.
    Laissez tout ce qui tombe
      Tomber !

Next, we may take two songs of earlier and later life, whose contrast is perfect concord.

I.

CHANSON D'AUTREFOIS.

    Jamais elle ne raille,
    Etant un calme esprit ;
    Mais toujours elle rit.—
Voici des brins de mousse avec des brins de paille ;
    Fauvette des roseaux,
    Fais ton nid sur les eaux.

    Quand sous la clarté douce
    Qui sort de tes beaux yeux
    On passe, on est joyeux.—
Voici des brins de paille avec des brins de mousse ;
    Martinet de l'azur,
    Fais ton nid dans mon mur.

Dans l'aube avril se mire,
Et les rameaux fleuris
Sont pleins de petits cris.—
Voici de son regard, voici de son sourire ;
Amour, ô doux vainqueur,
Fais ton nid dans mon cœur.

II.

CHANSON D'AUJOURD'HUI.

e disais :—Dieu qu'aucun suppliant n'importune,
Quand vous m'éprouverez dans votre volonté,
Laissez mon libre choix choisir dans la fortune
L'un ou l'autre côté ;

Entre un riche esclavage et la pauvreté franche
Laissez-moi choisir, Dieu du cèdre et du roseau ;
Entre l'or de la cage et le vert de la branche
Faites juge l'oiseau.—

Maintenant je suis libre et la nuit me réclame ;
J'ai choisi l'âpre exil ; j'habite un bois obscur ;
Mais je vois s'allumer les étoiles de l'âme
Dans mon sinistre azur.

If this can be surpassed for outward and inward sweetness, the following poem may perhaps have been equalled for sensible and spiritual terror in the range of lyric song.

EN MARCHANT LA NUIT DANS UN BOIS.

I.

Il grêle, il pleut.   Neige et brume ;
Fondrière à chaque pas.
Le torrent veut, crie, écume,
Et le rocher ne veut pas.

Le sabbat à notre oreille
Jette ses vagues hourras.
Un fagot sur une vieille
Passe en agitant les bras.

Passants hideux, clartés blanches ;
Il semble, en ces noirs chemins,
Que les hommes ont des branches,
Que les arbres ont des mains.

II.

On entend passer un coche,
Le lourd coche de la mort.
Il vient, il roule, il approche.
L'eau hurle et la bise mord.

Le dur cocher, dans la plaine
Aux aspects noirs et changeants,
Conduit sa voiture pleine
De toute sorte de gens.

Novembre souffle, la terre
Frémit, la bourrasque fond ;
Les flèches du sagittaire
Sifflent dans le ciel profond.

III.

—Cocher, d'où viens-tu ? dit l'arbre.
—Où vas-tu ? dit l'eau qui fuit.
Le cocher est fait de marbre
Et le coche est fait de nuit.

Il emporte beauté, gloire,
Joie, amour, plaisirs bruyants ;
La voiture est toute noire,
Les chevaux sont effrayants.

L'arbre en frissonnant s'incline.
L'eau sent les joncs se dresser.
Le buisson sur la colline
Grimpe pour le voir passer.

IV.

Le brin d'herbe sur la roche,
Le nuage dans le ciel,
Regarde marcher ce coche,
Et croit voir rouler Babel.

Sur sa morne silhouette,
Battant de l'aile à grands cris,
Volent l'orage, chouette,
Et l'ombre, chauve-souris.

Vent glacé, tu nous secoues !
Le char roule, et l'œil tremblant,
À travers ses grandes roues,
Voit un crépuscule blanc.

V.

La nuit, sinistre merveille,
Répand son effroi sacré ;
Toute la forêt s'éveille,
Comme un dormeur effaré.

Après les oiseaux, les âmes !
Volez sous les cieux blafards.
L'étang, miroir, rit aux femmes
Qui sortent des nénuphars.

L'air sanglote, et le vent râle,
Et, sous l'obscur firmament,
La nuit sombre et la mort pâle
Se regardent fixement.

But the twenty-fifth poem in this book of lyrics has assuredly never been excelled since first the impulse of articulate song awoke in the first recorded or unrecorded poet.

Proscrit, regarde les roses ;
Mai joyeux, de l'aube en pleurs
Les reçoit toutes écloses ;
Proscrit, regarde les fleurs.

    —Je pense
Aux roses que je semai.
Le mois de mai sans la France,
Ce n'est pas le mois de mai.

Proscrit, regarde les tombes ;
Mai, qui rit aux cieux si beaux,
Sous les baisers des colombes
Fait palpiter les tombeaux.

    —Je pense
Aux yeux chers que je fermai.
Le mois de mai sans la France,
Ce n'est pas le mois de mai.

Proscrit, regarde les branches,
Les branches où sont les nids ;
Mai les remplit d'ailes blanches
Et de soupirs infinis.

    —Je pense
Aux nids charmants où j'aimai.
Le mois de mai sans la France,
Ce n'est pas le mois de mai.

Mai 1854.

In October of the same year—the second year of his long
exile—a loftier note of no less heavenly melody was sounded
by the lyric poet who alone of all his nation has taken his
place beside Coleridge and Shelley. The word 'passant,'
as addressed by the soul to the body, is perhaps the very
finest expression of his fervent faith in immortality to be
found in all the work of Victor Hugo.

Il est un peu tard pour faire la belle,
Reine marguerite ; aux champs défleuris
Bientôt vont souffler le givre et la grêle.
— Passant, l'hiver vient, et je lui souris.

Il est un peu tard pour faire la belle,
Etoile du soir ; les rayons taris
Sont tous retournés à l'aube éternelle.
—Passant, la nuit vient, et je lui souris.

Il est un peu tard pour faire la belle,
Mon âme ; joyeuse en mes noirs débris,
Tu m'éblouis, fière et rouvrant ton aile.
—Passant, la mort vient, et je lui souris.

No date is affixed to the divine song of yearning after home and the graves which make holier for every man old enough to have been a mourner the native land which holds them. The play on sound which distinguishes the last repetition of the burden is the crowning evidence that the subtlest effect of pathos and the most austere effect of sublimity may be conveyed through a trick of language familiar in their highest and most serious moods to Æschylus and to Shakespeare.

EXIL.

Si je pouvais voir, ô patrie,
Tes amandiers et tes lilas,
Et fouler ton herbe fleurie,
          Hélas !

Si je pouvais,—mais, ô mon père,
O ma mère, je ne peux pas,—
Prendre pour chevet votre pierre,
          Hélas !

Dans le froid cercueil qui vous gêne,
Si je pouvais vous parler bas,
Mon frère Abel, mon frère Eugène,
          Hélas !

Si je pouvais, ô ma colombe,
Et toi, mère, qui t'envolas,
M'agenouiller sur votre tombe,
          Hélas !

Oh ! vers l'étoile solitaire,
Comme je lèverais les bras !
Comme je baiserais la terre,
          Hélas !

Loin de vous, ô morts que je pleure,
Des flots noirs j'écoute le glas ;
Je voudrais fuir, mais je demeure,
          Hélas !

Pourtant le sort, caché dans l'ombre,
Se trompe si, comptant mes pas,
Il croit que le vieux marcheur sombre
          Est las.

The epic book is the most tragic and terrible of all existing poems of its kind ; if indeed we may say that it properly
belongs to any kind existing before its advent.   The grow-
ing horror of the gradual vision of history, from Henri the
Fourth to his bloody and gloomy son, from Louis the Thirteenth to the murderer and hangman of the Palatinate and
the Cévennes, from Louis the Fourteenth to the inexpressible
pollution of incarnate ignominy in his grandson, seems to
heave and swell as a sea towards the coming thunder which
was to break above the severed head of their miserable
son.

And next year came *Torquemada* : one of the greatest
masterpieces of the master poet of our century.   The construction of this tragedy is absolutely original and unique :
free and full of change as the wildest and loosest and

roughest of dramatic structures ever flung together, and left
to crumble or cohere at the pleasure of accident or of luck, by
the rudest of primæval playwrights : but perfect in harmonious unity of spirit, in symmetry or symphony of part with
part, as the most finished and flawless creation of Sophocles
or of Phidias.   Between some of the characters in this play
and some of those in previous plays of Hugo's there is a
certain resemblance as of kinship, but no touch or shadow
of mere repetition or reproduction from types which had
been used before : Ferdinand the Catholic has something in
his lineaments of Louis the Just, and Gucho of L'Angely in
Marion de Lorme : the marquis of Fuentel has a touch of
Gunich in *Les deux trouvailles de Gallus*, redeemed by a
better touch of human tenderness for his recovered grandson.   The young lovers are two of the loveliest figures,
Torquemada is one of the sublimest, in all the illimitable
world of dramatic imagination.   The intensity of interest,
anxiety, and terror, which grows by such rapid and subtle
stages of development up to the thunderstroke of royal
decision at the close of the first act, is exchanged in the
second for an even deeper and higher kind of emotion.   The
confrontation of the hermit with the inquisitor, magnificent
enough already in its singleness of effect, is at once transfigured and completed by the apparition of the tremendous
figure whose very name is tragedy, whose very shadow
sufficed for the central and the crowning terror which darkened the stage of *Lucrèce Borgia*.

LE CHASSEUR.

Le hasard a pétri la cendre avec l'instant ;
Cet amalgame est l'homme.   Or, moi-même n'étant

Comme vous que matière, ah ! je serais stupide
D'être hésitant et lourd quand la joie est rapide,
De ne point mordre en hâte au plaisir dans la nuit,
Et de ne pas goûter à tout, puisque tout fuit !
Avant tout, être heureux. Je prends à mon service
Ce qu'on appelle crime et ce qu'on nomme vice.
L'inceste, préjugé. Le meurtre, expédient.
J'honore le scrupule en le congédiant.
Est-ce que vous croyez que, si ma fille est belle,
Je me gênerai, moi, pour être amoureux d'elle !
Ah ça, mais je serais un imbécile. Il faut
Que j'existe. Allez donc demander au gerfaut,
A l'aigle, à l'épervier, si cette chair qu'il broie
Est permise, et s'il sait de quel nid sort sa proie.
Parce que vous portez un habit noir ou blanc,
Vous vous croyez forcé d'être inepte et tremblant,
Et vous baissez les yeux devant cette offre immense
Du bonheur, que vous fait l'univers en démence.
Ayons donc de l'esprit. Profitons du temps. Rien
Etant le résultat de la mort, vivons bien !
La salle de bal croule et devient catacombe.
L'âme du sage arrive en dansant dans la tombe.
Servez-moi mon festin. S'il exige aujourd'hui
Un assaisonnement de poison pour autrui,
Soit. Qu'importe la mort des autres ! J'ai la vie.
Je suis une faim, vaste, ardente, inassouvie.
Mort, je veux t'oublier ; Dieu, je veux t'ignorer.
Oui, le monde est pour moi le fruit à dévorer.
Vivant, je suis en hâte heureux ; mort, je m'échappe !

   François de Paule, *à Torquemada.*

Qu'est-ce que ce bandit ?

     Torquemada.
      Mon père, c'est le pape.

The third act revives again the more immediate and
personal interest of the drama. Terror and pity never rose

higher, never found utterance more sublime and piercing, in any work of any poet in the world, than here in the scene of the supplication of the Jews, and the ensuing scene of the triumph of Torquemada.

The Jews enter ; men, women, and children all covered with ashes and clothed in rags, barefoot, with ropes round their necks, some mutilated and made infirm by torture, dragging themselves on crutches or on stumps ; others, whose eyes have been put out, are led by children. And their spokesman pleads thus with the king and the queen of the kingdoms from whence they are to be driven by Christian jurisdiction.

MOÏSE-BEN-HABIB, *grand rabbin, à genoux.*

Altesse de Castille, altesse d'Aragon,
Roi, reine ! ô notre maître, et vous, notre maîtresse,
Nous, vos tremblants sujets, nous sommes en détresse,
Et, pieds nus, corde au cou, nous prions Dieu d'abord,
Et vous ensuite, étant dans l'ombre de la mort,
Ayant plusieurs de nous qu'on va livrer aux flammes,
Et tout le reste étant chassé, vieillards et femmes,
Et, sous l'œil qui voit tout du fond du firmament,
Rois, nous vous apportons notre gémissement.
Altesses, vos décrets sur nous se précipitent,
Nous pleurons, et les os de nos pères palpitent ;
Le sépulcre pensif tremble à cause de vous.
Ayez pitié. Nos cœurs sont fidèles et doux ;
Nous vivons enfermés dans nos maisons étroites,
Humbles, seuls ; nos lois sont très simples et très droites,
Tellement qu'un enfant les mettrait en écrit.
Jamais le juif ne chante et jamais il ne rit.
Nous payons le tribut, n'importe quelles sommes.
On nous remue à terre avec le pied ; nous sommes

Comme le vêtement d'un homme assassiné.

Gloire à Dieu ! Mais faut-il qu' avec le nouveau-né,
Avec l'enfant qu'on tette, avec l'enfant qu'on sèvre,
Nu, poussant devant lui son chien, son bœuf, sa chèvre,
Israël fuie et coure épars dans tous les sens !
Qu'on ne soit plus un peuple et qu'on soit des passants !
Rois, ne nous faites pas chasser à coups de piques,
Et Dieu vous ouvrira des portes magnifiques.
Ayez pitié de nous. Nous sommes accablés.
Nous ne verrons donc plus nos arbres et nos blés !
Les mères n'auront plus de lait dans leurs mamelles !
Les bêtes dans les bois sont avec leurs femelles,
Les nids dorment heureux sous les branches blottis,
On laisse en paix la biche allaiter ses petits,
Permettez-nous de vivre aussi, nous, dans nos caves,
Sous nos pauvres toits, presque au bagne et presque
    esclaves,
Mais auprès des cercueils de nos pères ! daignez
Nous souffrir sous vos pieds de nos larmes baignés !
Oh ! la dispersion sur les routes lointaines,
Quel deuil ! Permettez-nous de boire à nos fontaines
Et de vivre en nos champs, et vous prospérerez.
Hélas ! nous nous tordons les bras, désespérés !
Épargnez-nous l'exil, ô rois, et l'agonie
De la solitude âpre, éternelle, infinie !
Laissez-nous la patrie et laissez-nous le ciel !
Le pain sur qui l'on pleure en mangeant est du fiel.
Ne soyez pas le vent si nous sommes la cendre.
Voici notre rançon, hélas ! daignez la prendre.
O rois, protégez-nous. Voyez nos désespoirs.
Soyez sur nous, mais non comme des anges noirs ;
Soyez des anges bons et doux, car l'aile sombre
Et l'aile blanche, ô rois, ne font pas la même ombre.
Révoquez votre arrêt. Rois, nous vous supplions
Par vos aïeux sacrés, grands comme les lions,
Par les tombeaux des rois, par les tombeaux des reines,
Profonds et pénétrés de lumières sereines,

Et nous mettons nos cœurs, ô maîtres des humains,
Nos prières, nos deuils dans les petites mains
De votre infante Jeanne, innocente, et pareille
À la fraise des bois où se pose l'abeille.
Roi, reine, ayez pitié !

After the sublime and inexpressible pathos of this
appeal from age and innocence against the most execrable of
all religions that ever infected earth and verified hell, it
would have been impossible for any poet but one to find
expression for the passion of unselfish faith in that in-
fernal creed which should not merely horrify and disgust us.
But when Hugo brings before us the figure of the grand
inquisitor in contemplation of the supreme act of faith accomplished in defiance of king and queen to the greater glory
of God, for the ultimate redemption of souls else condemned to everlasting torment, the rapture of the terrible
redeemer, whose faith is in salvation by fire, is rendered into
words of such magical and magnificent inspiration that the
conscience of our fancy is wellnigh conquered and convinced
and converted for the moment as we read.

TORQUEMADA.

O fête, ô gloire, ô joie !
La clémence terrible et superbe flamboie !
Délivrance à jamais !   Damnés, soyez absous !
Le bûcher sur la terre éteint l'enfer dessous.
Sois béni, toi par qui l'âme au bonheur remonte,
Bûcher, gloire du feu dont l'enfer est la honte,
Issue aboutissant au radieux chemin,
Porte du paradis rouverte au genre humain,
Miséricorde ardente aux caresses sans nombre,
Mystérieux rachat des esclaves de l'ombre,

Auto-da-fé ! Pardon, bonté, lumière, feu,
Vie ! éblouissement de la face de Dieu !
Oh ! quel départ splendide et que d'âmes sauvées !
Juifs, mécréants, pécheurs, ô mes chères couvées,
Un court tourment vous paie un bonheur infini ;
L'homme n'est plus maudit, l'homme n'est plus banni ;
Le salut s'ouvre au fond des cieux. L'amour s'éveille,
Et voici son triomphe, et voici sa merveille !
Quelle extase ! entrer droit au ciel ! ne pas languir !

       Cris dans le brasier.

Entendez-vous Satan hurler de les voir fuir ?
Que l'éternel forçat pleure en l'éternel bouge !
J'ai poussé de mes poings l'énorme porte rouge.
Oh ! comme il a grincé lorsque je refermais
Sur lui les deux battants hideux, Toujours, Jamais !
Sinistre, il est resté derrière le mur sombre.

       Il regarde le ciel.

Oh ! j'ai pansé la plaie effrayante de l'ombre.
Le paradis souffrait ; le ciel avait au flanc
Cet ulcère, l'enfer brûlant, l'enfer sanglant ;
J'ai posé sur l'enfer la flamme bienfaitrice,
Et j'en vois dans l'immense azur la cicatrice.
C'était ton coup de lance au côté, Jésus-Christ !
Hosanna ! la blessure éternelle guérit.
Plus d'enfer. C'est fini. Les douleurs sont taries.

       Il regarde le quemadero.

Rubis de la fournaise ! ô braises ! pierreries !
Flambez, tisons ! brûlez, charbons ! feu souverain,
Pétille ! luis, bûcher ! prodigieux écrin
D'étincelles qui vont devenir des étoiles !
Les âmes, hors des corps comme hors de leurs voiles,
S'en vont, et le bonheur sort du bain de tourments !
Splendeur ! magnificence ardente ! flamboiements !
Satan, mon ennemi, qu'en dis-tu ?

       En extase.

         Feu ! lavage
De toutes les noirceurs par la flamme sauvage !

Transfiguration suprême ! acte de foi !
Nous sommes deux sous l'œil de Dieu, Satan et moi.
Deux porte-fourches, lui, moi.   Deux maîtres des flammes.
Lui perdant les humains, moi secourant les âmes ;
Tous deux bourreaux, faisant par le même moyen
Lui l'enfer, moi le ciel, lui le mal, moi le bien ;
Il est dans le cloaque et je suis dans le temple,
Et le noir tremblement de l'ombre nous contemple.

            Il se retourne vers les suppliciés.

Ah ! sans moi, vous étiez perdus, mes bien-aimés !
La piscine de feu vous épure enflammés.
Ah ! vous me maudissez pour un instant qui passe,
Enfants ! mais tout à l'heure, oui, vous me rendrez grâce
Quand vous verrez à quoi vous avez échappé ;
Car, ainsi que Michel-Archange, j'ai frappé ;
Car les blancs séraphins, penchés au puits de soufre,
Raillent le monstrueux avortement du gouffre ;
Car votre hurlement de haine arrive au jour,
Bégaie, et, stupéfait, s'achève en chant d'amour !
Oh ! comme j'ai souffert de vous voir dans les chambres
De torture, criant, pleurant, tordant vos membres,
Maniés par l'étau d'airain, par le fer chaud !
Vous voilà délivrés, partez, fuyez là-haut !
Entrez au paradis !

            Il se penche et semble regarder sous terre.

                        Non, tu n'auras plus d'âmes !

      Il se redresse.

Dieu nous donne l'appui que nous lui demandâmes,
Et l'homme est hors du gouffre.   Allez, allez, allez !
A travers l'ombre ardente et les grands feux ailés,
L'évanouissement de la fumée emporte
Là-haut l'esprit vivant sauvé de la chair morte !
Tout le vieux crime humain de l'homme est arraché ;
L'un avait son erreur, l'autre avait son péché,
Faute ou vice, chaque âme avait son monstre en elle
Qui rongeait sa lumière et qui mordait son aile ;
L'ange expirait en proie au démon.   Maintenant
Tout brûle, et le partage auguste et rayonnant

Se fait devant Jésus dans la clarté des tombes.
Dragons, tombez en cendre ; envolez-vous, colombes !
Vous que l'enfer tenait, liberté ! liberté !
Montez de l'ombre au jour.   Changez d'éternité !

The last act would indeed be too cruel for endurance if it were not too beautiful for blame.   But not the inquisition itself was more inevitably inexorable than is the spiritual law, the unalterable and immitigable instinct, of tragic poetry at its highest.   Dante could not redeem Francesca, Shakespeare could not rescue Cordelia.   To none of us, we must think, can the children of a great poet's divine imagination seem dearer or more deserving of mercy than they seemed to their creator : but when poetry demands their immolation, they must die, that they may live for ever.

Once more, but now for the last time, the world was to receive yet another gift from the living hand of the greatest man it had seen since Shakespeare.   Towards the close of his eighty-second year he bestowed on us the crowning volume of his crowning work, the imperishable and inappreciable *Légende des Siècles*.   And at the age of eighty-three years, two months, and twenty-six days, he entered into rest for ever, and into glory which can perish only with the memory of all things memorable among all races and nations of mankind.

I have spoken here—and no man can know so well or feel so deeply as myself with what imperfection of utterance and inadequacy of insight I have spoken—of Victor Hugo as the whole world knew and as all honourable or intelligent men regarded and revered him.   But there are those among his friends and mine who would have a right to wonder if no word were here to be said of the unsolicited and unmerited kindness which first vouchsafed to take notice of a crude and puerile attempt to render some tribute of thanks for the gifts of his genius just twenty-three years ago ; of the kindness which was always but too ready to recognize and requite a gratitude which had no claim on him but that of a very perfect loyalty ; of the kindness which many years afterwards received me as a guest under his roof with the welcome of a father to a son. Such matters, if touched on at all, unquestionably should not be dwelt on in public : but to give them no word whatever of acknowledgment at parting would show rather unthankfulness than reserve in one who was honoured so far above all possible hope or merit by the paternal goodness of Victor Hugo.

1885.

LA LÉGENDE DES SIÈCLES

1883.

'Chacun a sa manière. Quant à moi, qui parle ici, j'admire tout, comme une brute.—N'espérez donc aucune critique.—Je ne chicane point ces grands bienfaiteurs-là. Ce que vous qualifiez défaut, je le qualifie accent. Je reçois et je remercie.—Ayant eu l'honneur d'être appelé " niais " par plusieurs écrivains et critiques distingués, je cherche à justifier l'épithète.'

THE greatest work of the century is now at length complete. It is upwards of twenty-four years since the first part of it was sent home to France from Guernsey. Eighteen years later we received a second instalment of the yet unexhausted treasure. And here, at the age of eighty-one, the sovereign poet of the world has placed the copingstone on the stateliest of spiritual buildings that ever in modern times has been reared for the wonder and the worship of mankind.

Those only to whom nothing seems difficult because nothing to them seems greater than themselves could find it other than an arduous undertaking to utter some word of not unworthy welcome and thanksgiving when their life is suddenly enriched and brightened by such an addition to its most precious things as the dawn of a whole new world of song—and a world that may hold its own in heaven beside the suns created or evoked by the fiat of Shakespeare or of Dante. To review the *Divine Comedy*, to dispose of *Hamlet* in the course of a leading article, to despatch in a few sentences the question of *Paradise Lost* and its claim to immortality, might seem easy to judges who should feel themselves on a level with the givers of these gifts ; for others it could be none the less difficult to discharge this office because the gift was but newly given. One minor phase of the difficulty which presents itself is this : the temporary judge, self-elected to pass sentence on any supreme achievement of human power, must choose on which horn of an inevitable dilemma he may prefer to run the risk of impalement. If, recognising in this new master-work an equal share of the highest qualities possible to man with that possessed and manifested by any previous writer of now unquestioned supremacy, he takes upon himself to admit, simply and honestly, that he does recognise this, and cannot choose but recognise it, he must know that his judgment will be received with no more tolerance or respect, with no less irritation and derision, than would have been, in Dante's time, the judgment of a critic who should have ventured to rank Dante above Virgil, in Shakespeare's time of a critic who should have dared to set Shakespeare beside Homer. If, on the other hand, he should abstain with all due discretion from any utterance or any intimation of a truth so ridiculous and untimely, he runs the sure and certain risk of leaving behind him a name to be ranked, by all who remember it at all, with those which no man mentions without a smile of compassion or of scorn, according to the quality of error discernible in the critic's misjudgment : innocent and incurable

as the confidence of a Johnson or a Jeffrey, venomous
and malignant as the rancour of Sainte-Beuve or Gifford.
Of these two dangers I choose the former ; and venture to
admit, in each case with equal diffidence, that I do upon the
whole prefer Dante to any Cino or Cecco, Shakespeare to
all the Greenes and Peeles and Lillys, Victor Hugo to all
or any, of their respective times. The reader who has no
tolerance for paradox or presumption has therefore fair
warning to read no further.

Auguste Vacquerie, of all poets and all men living the
most worthy to praise the greatest poet of his century, has
put on record long ago, with all the vivid ardour of his admirable style, an experience of which I now am but too
forcibly reminded. He was once invited by Victor Hugo
to choose among the manuscripts of the master's unpublished
work, from the drawers containing respectively some lyric or
dramatic or narrative masterpiece, of which among the three
kinds he would prefer to have a sample first. Unable to
select, he touched a drawer at random, which contained the
opening chapters of a yet unfinished story—*Les Misérables.*
If it is no less hard to choose where to begin in a notice of
the *Légende des Siècles*—to decide what star in all this
thronged and living heaven should first attract the direction
of our critical telescope—it is on the other hand no less
certain that on no side can the telescope be misdirected.
From the miraculous music of a legendary dawn, when the
first woman felt first within her the movement of her first-
born child, to the crowning vision of ultimate justice made
visible and material in the likeness of the trumpet of doom,
no radiance or shadow of days or nights intervening, no
change of light or cadence of music in all the tragic pageant

of the centuries, finds less perfect expression and response less absolute refraction or reflection, than all that come and go before or after it. History and legend, fact and vision, are fused and harmonised by the mastering charm of moral unity in imaginative truth. There is no more possibility of discord or default in this transcendent work of human power than in the working of those powers of nature which transcend humanity. In the first verses of the overture we hear such depth and height of music, see such breadth and splendour of beauty, that we know at once these cannot but continue to the end ; and from the end, when we arrive at the goal of the last line, we look back and perceive that it has been so. Were this overture but a thought less perfect, a shade less triumphant, we might doubt if what was to follow it could be as perfect and triumphant as itself. We might begin—and indeed, as it is, there are naturally those who have begun—to debate with ourselves or to dispute with the poet as to the details of his scheme, the selection of his types, the propriety of his method, the accuracy of his title. There are those who would seem to infer from the choice of this title that the book is, in the most vulgar sense, of a purely legendary cast ; who object, for example, that a record of unselfish and devoted charity shown by the poor to the poor is, happily, no 'legend.' Writers in whom such self-exposure of naked and unashamed ignorance with respect to the rudiments of language is hardly to be feared have apparently been induced or inclined to expect some elaborate and orderly review of history, some versified chronicle of celebrated events and significant epochs, such as might perhaps be of subsidiary or supplementary service in the training of candidates for a competitive examination ; and

on finding something very different from this have tossed
head and shrugged shoulder in somewhat mistimed im-
patience, as at some deception or misnomer on the great
author's part which they, as men of culture and understanding, had a reasonable right to resent. The book, they affirm,
is a mere agglomeration of unconnected episodes, irrelevant
and incoherent, disproportionate and fortuitous, chosen at
random by accident or caprice ; it is not one great palace
of poetry, but a series or congeries rather of magnificently
accumulated fragments. It may be urged in answer to this
impeachment that the unity of the book is not logical but
spiritual ; its diversity is not accidental or chaotic, it is the
result and expression of a spontaneous and perfect harmony,
as clear and as profound as that of the other greatest works
achieved by man. To demonstrate this by rule and line of
syllogism is no present ambition of mine. A humbler, a
safer, and perhaps a more profitable task would be to
attempt some flying summary, some glancing revision of
the three great parts which compose this mightiest poem of
our age ; or rather, if this also should seem too presumptuous an aspiration, to indicate here and there the points
to which memory and imagination are most fain to revert
most frequently and brood upon them longest, with a
deeper delight, a more rapturous reverence, than waits upon
the rest. Not that I would venture to assert or to insinuate
that there is in any poem of the cycle any note whatever of
inferiority or disparity ; but having neither space nor time
nor power to speak, however inadequately, of each among
the hundred and thirty-eight poems which compose the
now perfect book, I am compelled to choose, not quite at
random, an example here and there of its highest and most

typical qualities. In the first book, for instance, of the first series, the divine poem on Ruth and Boaz may properly be taken as representative of that almost indefinable quality which hitherto has seemed more especially the gift of Dante : a fusion, so to speak, of sublimity with sweetness, the exaltation of loveliness into splendour and simplicity into mystery, such as glorifies the close of his *Purgatory* and the opening of his *Paradise*. Again, the majestic verses which bring Mahomet before us at his end strike a deeper impression into the memory than is left by the previous poem on the raising of Lazarus ; and when we pass into the cycle of heroic or chivalrous legend we find those poems the loftiest and the loveliest which have in them most of that prophetic and passionate morality which makes the greatest poet, in this as in some other ages, as much a seer as a singer, an evangelist no less than an artist. Hugo, for all his dramatic and narrative mastery of effect, will always probably remind men rather of such poets as Dante or Isaiah than of such poets as Sophocles or Shakespeare. We cannot of course imagine the Florentine or the Hebrew endowed with his infinite variety of sympathies, of interests, and of powers ; but as little can we imagine in the Athenian such height and depth of passion, in the Englishman such unquenchable and sleepless fire of moral and prophetic faith. And hardly in any one of these, though Shakespeare may perhaps be excepted, can we recognise the same buoyant and childlike exultation in such things as are the delight of a high-hearted child—in free glory of adventure and ideal daring, in the triumph and rapture of reinless imagination, which gives now and then some excess of godlike empire and super-human kingship to their hands whom his hands have

created, to the lips whose life is breathed into them from
his own. By the Homeric stature of the soul he measures
the heroic capacity of the sword. And indeed it is hardly in
our century that men who do not wish to provoke laughter
should venture to mock at a poet who puts a horde to
flight before a hero, or strikes down strongholds by the
lightning of a single will. No right and no power to dis-
believe in the arm of Hercules or the voice of Jesus can
rationally remain with those who have seen Garibaldi take
a kingdom into the hollow of his hand, and not one man
but a whole nation arise from the dead at the sound of the
word of Mazzini.

Two out of the five heroic poems which compose the
fourth book of the first series will always remain types of
what the genius of Hugo could achieve in two opposite
lines. All the music of morning, all the sunshine of
romance, all the sweetness and charm of chivalry, will come
back upon all readers at the gracious and radiant name of
Aymerillot ; all the blackness of darkness, rank with fumes
of blood and loud with cries of torment, which covers in so
many quarters the history, not romantic but actual, of the
ages called ages of faith, will close in upon the memory
which reverts to the direful *Day of Kings*. The sound of
the final note struck in the latter poem remains in the
mind as the echo of a crowning peal of thunder in the
ear of one entranced and spell-stricken by the magnetism of
storm. The Pyrenees belong to Hugo as the western coasts
of Italy, Neapolitan or Tuscan, belong to Shelley ; they can
never again be done into words and translated into music
as for once they have been by these. It can hardly be said
that he who knows the Pyrenees has read Victor Hugo ;

but certainly it may be said that he who knows Victor Hugo has seen the Pyrenees. From the author's prefatory avowal that his book contains few bright or smiling pictures, a reader would never have inferred that so many of its pages are fragrant with all the breath and radiant with all the bloom of April or May among the pine-woods and their mountain lawns, ablaze with ardent blossom and astir with triumphant song. Tragedy may be hard at hand, with all the human train of sorrows and passions and sins ; but the glory of beauty, the loveliness of love, the exultation of noble duty and lofty labour in a stress of arduous joy, these are the influences that pervade the world and permeate the air of the poems which deal with the Christian cycle of heroic legend, whose crowning image is the ideal figure of the Cid. To this highest and purest type of mediæval romance or history the fancy of the great poet whose childhood was cradled in Spain turns and returns throughout the course of his threefold masterpiece with an almost national pride and passion of sublime delight. Once in the first part and once in the third his chosen hero is set before us in heroic verse, doing menial service for his father in his father's house, and again, in a king's palace, doing for humanity the sovereign service of tyrannicide. But in the second part it seems as though the poet could hardly, with his fullest effusion of lyric strength and sweetness, do enough to satisfy his loving imagination of the perfect knight, most faithful and most gentle and most terrible, whom he likens even to the very Pic du Midi in its majesty of solitude. Each fresh blast of verse has in it the ring of a golden clarion which proclaims in one breath the honour of the loyal soldier and the dishonour of the disloyal king. There can hardly be in any language a more precious and wonderful study of technical art in verse of the highest kind of simplicity than this *Romancero du Cid*, with its jet of luminous and burning song sustained without lapse or break through sixteen ' fyttes ' of plain brief ballad metre.   It is hard to say whether the one only master of all forms and kinds of poetry that ever left to all time the proof of his supremacy in all has shown most clearly by his use of its highest or his use of its simplest forms the innate and absolute equality of the French language as an instrument for poetry with the Greek of Æschylus and of Sappho, the English of Milton and of Shelley.

But among all Hugo's romantic and tragic poems of mediæval history or legend the two greatest are in my mind *Eviradnus* and *Ratbert*.   I cannot think it would be rash to assert that the loveliest love-song in the world, the purest and keenest rapture of lyric fancy, the sweetest and clearest note of dancing or dreaming music, is that which rings for ever in the ear which has once caught the matchless echo of such lines as these that must once more be quoted, as though all the world of readers had not long since known them by heart :—

> Viens, sois tendre, je suis ivre.
> O les verts taillis mouillés !
> Ton souffle te fera suivre
> Des papillons réveillés.

> .   .   .   .   .

> Allons-nous-en par l'Autriche !
> Nous aurons l'aube à nos fronts ;
> Je serai grand, et toi riche,
> Puisque nous nous aimerons.

> .   .   .   .   .

Tu seras dame, et moi comte ;
Viens, mon cœur s'épanouit,
Viens, nous conterons ce conte
Aux étoiles de la nuit.

The poet would be as sure of a heavenly immortality in the hearts of men as any lyrist of Greece itself, who should only have written the fourteen stanzas of the song from which I have ventured to choose these three.   All the sounds and shadows of a moonlit wilderness, all the dews and murmurs and breaths of midsummer midnight, have become for once articulate in such music as was never known even to Shakespeare's forest of Arden.   In the heart of a poem so full of tragedy and terror that Hugo alone could have brightened it with his final touch of sunrise, this birdlike rapture breaks out as by some divine effect of unforbidden and blameless magic.

And yet, it may be said or thought, the master of masters has shown himself even greater in *Ratbert* than in *Eviradnus*.   This most tragic of poems, lit up by no such lyric interlude, stands unsurpassed even by its author for tenderness, passion, divine magnificence of righteous wrath, august and pitiless command of terror and pity.   From the kingly and priestly conclave of debaters more dark than Milton's to the superb admonition of loyal liberty in speech that can only be silenced by murder, and again from the heavenly and heroic picture of childhood worshipped by old age to the monstrous banquet of massacre, when the son of the prostitute has struck his perjured stroke of state, the poem passes through a change of successive pageants each fuller of splendour and wonder, of loveliness or of horror, than the last.   But the agony of the hero over the little

corpse of the child murdered with her plaything in her hand
—the anguish that utters itself as in peal upon peal of
thunder, broken by sobs of storm—the full crash of the
final imprecation, succeeded again by such unspeakably
sweet and piteous appeal to the little dead lips and eyes that
would have answered yesterday—and at last the one crowning stroke of crime which calls down an answering stroke
of judgment from the very height of heaven, for the comfort
and refreshment and revival of all hearts—these are things
of which no praise can speak aright.   Shakespeare only,
were he living, would be worthy to write on Hugo's Fabrice
as Hugo has written on Shakespeare's Lear.   History will
forget the name of Bonaparte before humanity forgets the
name of Ratbert.

But if this be the highest poem of all for passion and
pathos and fire of terrible emotion, the highest in sheer sublimity of imagination is to my mind *Zim-Zizimi.*   Again and
again, in reading it for the first time, one thinks that surely
now the utmost height is reached, the utmost faculty revealed,
that can be possible for a spirit clothed only with human
powers, armed only with human speech.   And always one
finds the next step forward to be yet once more a step up-
ward, even to the very end and limit of them all.   Neither in
Homer nor in Milton, nor in the English version of Job or
Ezekiel or Isaiah, is the sound of the roll and surge of
measured music more wonderful than here.   Even after the
vision of the tomb of Belus the miraculous impression of
splendour and terror, distinct in married mystery, and
diverse in unity of warning, deepens and swells onward like
a sea till we reach the incomparable psalm in praise of the
beauty and the magic of womanhood made perfect and

made awful in Cleopatra, which closes in horror at the
touch of a hand more powerful than Orcagna's.   The walls
of the Campo Santo are fainter preachers and feebler pur-
suivants of the triumph of death than the pages of the poem
which yet again renews its note of menace after menace and
prophecy upon prophecy till the end.   There is probably not
one single couplet in all this sweet and bitter roll of song
which could have been written by any poet less than the
best or lower than the greatest of all time.

> Passants, quelqu'un veut-il voir Cléopâtre au lit ?
> Venez ; l'alcôve est morne, une brume l'emplit ;
> Cléopâtre est couchée à jamais ; cette femme
> Fut l'éblouissement de l'Asie, et la flamme
> Que tout le genre humain avait dans son regard ;
> Quand elle disparut, le monde fut hagard ;
> Ses dents étaient de perle et sa bouche était d'ambre ;
> Les rois mouraient d'amour en entrant dans sa chambre ;
> Pour elle Ephractæus soumit l'Atlas, Sapor
> Vint d'Ozymandias saisir le cercle d'or,
> Mamylos conquit Suse et Tentyris détruite
> Et Palmyre, et pour elle Antoine prit la fuite ;
> Entre elle et l'univers qui s'offraient à la fois
> Il hésita, lâchant le monde dans son choix.
> Cléopâtre égalait les Junons éternelles ;
> Une chaîne sortait de ses vagues prunelles ;
> O tremblant cœur humain, si jamais tu vibras,
> C'est dans l'étreinte altière et douce de ses bras ;
> Son nom seul enivrait ; Strophus n'osait l'écrire ;
> La terre s'éclairait de son divin sourire,
> À force de lumière et d'amour, effrayant ;
> Son corps semblait mêlé d'azur ; en la voyant,
> Vénus, le soir, rentrait jalouse sous la nue ;
> Cléopâtre embaumait l'Egypte ; toute nue,
> Elle brûlait les yeux ainsi que le soleil ;
> Les roses enviaient l'ongle de son orteil ;

O vivants, allez voir sa tombe souveraine ;
Fière, elle était déesse et daignait être reine ;
L'amour prenait pour arc sa lèvre aux coins moqueurs ;
Sa beauté rendait fous les fronts, les sens, les cœurs,
Et plus que les lions rugissants était forte ;
Mais bouchez-vous le nez si vous passez la porte.

At every successive stage of his task, the man who un-
dertakes to glance over this great cycle of poems must
needs incessantly call to mind the most worn and hackneyed
of all quotations from its author's works—'J'en passe, et
des meilleurs.' There is here no room, as surely there
should nowhere now be any need, to speak at any length of
the poems in which Roland plays the part of protagonist ;
first as the beardless champion of a five days' fight, and
again as the deliverer whose hand could clear the world of
a hundred human wolves in one continuous sword-sweep.
There is hardly time allowed us for one poor word or
two of tribute to such a crowning flower of song as *La
Rose de l'Infante*, with its parable of the broken Armada
made manifest in a wrecked fleet of drifting petals ; to the
superb and sonorous chant of the buccaneers, in which all
the noise of lawless battle and stormy laughter passes off
into the carol of mere triumphant love and trust ; or even
to the whole inner cycle of mystic and primæval legend
which seeks utterance for the human sense of oppression or
neglect by jealous or by joyous gods ; for the wild profound
revolt of riotous and trampled nature, the agony and passion and triumph of invincible humanity, the protest and
witness of enduring earth against the passing shades of
heaven, the struggle and the plea of eternal manhood
against all transient forces of ephemeral and tyrannous god-

head. Within the orbit of this epicycle one poem only of
the first part, a star of strife and struggle, can properly be
said to revolve ; but the light of that planet has fire enough
to animate with its reflex the whole concourse of stormy
stars which illuminate the world-wide wrestle of the giants
with the gods. The torch of revolt borne by the transfigured satyr, eyed like a god and footed like a beast, kindles
the lamp of hopeful and laborious rebellion which dazzles
us in the eye of the Titan who has seen beyond the world.
In the song that struck silence through the triumph of
amazed Olympus there is a sound and air as of the sea or
the Book of Job. There may be something of Persian or
Indian mysticism, there is more of universal and imaginative reason, in the great allegoric myth which sets forth
here how the half-brute child of one poor planet has in him
the seed, the atom, the principle of life everlasting, and
dilates in force of it to the very type and likeness of the
eternal universal substance which is spirit or matter of life ;
and before the face of his transfiguration the omnipresent
and omnipotent gods who take each their turn to shine and
thunder are all but shadows that pass away. Since the
Lord answered Job out of the whirlwind no ear has heard
the burst of such a song; but this time it is the world that
answers out of its darkness the lords and gods of creed and
oracle, who have mastered and have not made it. And
in the cry of its protest and the prophecy of its advance
there is a storm of swelling music which is as the sound
of the strength of rollers after the noise of the rage of
breakers.

It is noticeable that the master of modern poets should
have in the tone and colour of his genius more even of the

Hebrew than the Greek. In his love of light and freedom, reason and justice, he is not of Jerusalem, but of Athens ; but in the bent of his imagination, in the form and colour of his dreams, in the scope and sweep of his wide-winged spiritual flight, he is nearer akin to the great insurgent prophets of deliverance and restoration than to any poet of Athens except only their kinsman Æschylus. It is almost wholly of the Persian war, the pass of Thermopylæ, the strait of Euripus, that he sings when he sings of Hellas. All his might of hand, all his cunning of colour, all his measureless resources of sound and form and symbol, are put forth in the catalogue of nations and warriors subject to Xerxes. There is nothing in poetry so vast and tremendous of its kind as this pageant of immense and monstrous invasion. But indeed the choice of gigantic themes, the predominance of colossal effects, the prevalence of superhuman visions over the types and figures of human history or legend, may be regarded as a distinctive point of difference between the second and the first series. A typical example of the second is the poem which has added an eighth wonder built by music to the seven wonders of the world, which it celebrates in verse more surely wrought for immortality than they. Another is the song of the worm which takes up in answer to their chant of life and light and pride of place, and prolongs through measure after measure of rolling and reverberating verse, the note of a funereal and universal triumph, the protest and the proclamation of death. Another, attuned to that mighty music of meditation which rings through so many of the poems written in exile and loneliness, is the stately prophetic hymn which bears the superscription of *All the Past and all the Future*. This might seem to belong

to the sixth book of the *Contemplations*, in which the same
note of proud and ardent faith was struck so often with such
sovereignty of hand.   As much might be said of the great
' abysmal ' poem which closes the second series with a symphony of worlds and spirits.   Other groups of poems, in like
manner, bear signs of common or of diverse kinship to former
works of a creator whose spirit has put life into so many of
the same likeness, yet with no more sign of repetition or weary
monotony than is traceable in the very handiwork of nature.
The book of idyls is of one inspiration with the *Chansons
des Rues et des Bois* ; in both cases, as in so many of the
poet's earlier lyric volumes, his incomparable fertility of
speech and superb facility of verse leave almost an impression as of work done by way of exercise, as though he were
writing to keep his hand in, or to show for a wager with in-
credulous criticism how long he could keep up the golden ball
of metre, carve arabesques of the same pattern, play variations
in the same key.   But the *Old Man's Idyl* which closes the
book belongs by kinship to another work of the poet's, more
beloved and more precious to the inmost heart, if not more
eminent for strength and cunning of hand, than any of these.
In ' the voice of a child a year old ' there is the same welling
and bubbling melody which flows and laughs and murmurs
and glitters through the adorable verses of *L'Art d'être Grand-
père*, making dim with love and delight the reader's or the
hearer's eyes.   At last the language of babies has found its
interpreter ; and that, as might have been expected, in the
greatest poet of his age.

> L'enfant apporte un peu de ce ciel dont il sort ;
> Il ignore, il arrive ; homme, tu le recueilles.
> Il a le tremblement des herbes et des feuilles.

> La jaserie avant le langage est la fleur
> Qui précède le fruit, moins beau qu'elle, et meilleur,
> Si c'est être meilleur qu'être plus nécessaire.

A conclusion which may be doubted when we consider as follows :—

> L'enfant fait la demande et l'ange la réponse ;
> Le babil puéril dans le ciel bleu s'enfonce,
> Puis s'en revient, avec les hésitations
> Du moineau qui verrait planer les alcyons.

Can language or can thought be lovelier? if so, the one possible instance is to be sought in these succeeding verses :—

> Quand l'enfant jase avec l'ombre qui le bénit,
> La fauvette, attentive, au rebord de son nid
> Se dresse, et ses petits passent, pensifs et frêles,
> Leurs têtes à travers les plumes de ses ailes ;
> La mère semble dire à sa couvée : Entends,
> Et tâche de parler aussi bien.

It seems and is not strange that the lips which distil such honey as this should be the same so often touched with a coal of fire from that 'altar of Righteousness' where Æschylus was wont to worship. The twenty-first section of the second series is in the main a renewal or completion of the work undertaken in the immortal *Châtiments*. Even in that awful and incomparable book of judgment such poems as *La Colère du Bronze*, and the two following on the traffic of servile clerical rapacity in matters of death and burial, would have stood high among the stately legions of satire which fill its living pages with the sound and the splendour of righteous battle for the right ; but the verses with which Hugo has branded the betrayer of Metz and Strasburg are hardly to be matched except by those with which, half a century ago, he branded the betrayer of the Duchess of Berry. Truly may all who read them cry out with the poet at their close,

> Et qui donc maintenant dit qu'il s'est évadé ?

In *Le Cimetière d'Eylau*, a poem to which we have now in the third series of the book a most noble and exquisite pendant (*Paroles de mon Oncle*), all the Homeric side of a poet born of warlike blood comes out into proud and bright relief. There is no better fighting in the Iliad ; it has the martial precision and practical fellow-feeling which animate in his battle-pieces the lagging verse of Walter Scott ; and it has of course that omnipresent breath and light and fire of perfect poetry which a Scott or a Byron is never quite permitted to attain. Beside or even above these two poems, that other which commemorates the devotion of a Vendean peasant chief will be set in the hearts of all readers competent to appreciate either heroic action or heroic song.

The love of all high things which finds one form of expression in warlike sympathy with warriors who can live and die for something higher than personal credit or success takes another and as natural a shape in the poems which are inspired by love and worship of nature and her witness for liberty and purity and truth in the epic evangel of august and indomitable mountains. The sublimest cry of moral passion ever inspired by communion in spirit with these is uttered in the great poem on the Swiss mercenaries of the seventeenth century, which even among its fellows stands out eminent and radiant as an Alp at sunrise.

Mountain and cataract, the stars and the snows, never yet
in any language found such a singer and interpreter as this.
Two or three verses, two or three words, suffice for him to
bring before us, in fresh and actual presence, the very
breath of the hills or the sea, the very lights and sounds
and spaces of clouded or sunlit air. Juvenal is not so
strong in righteousness, nor Pindar so sublime in illustration, as the poet who borrowed from nature her highest
symbols to illustrate the glory and the duty of righteous
wrath and insuppressible insurrection against wrong-doing,
when he wrote *Le Régiment du baron Madruce*.

> L'homme s'est vendu. Soit. A-t-on dans le louage
> Compris le lac, le bois, la ronce, le nuage ?
> La nature revient, germe, fleurit, dissout,
> Féconde, croît, décroît, rit, passe, efface tout.
> La Suisse est toujours là, libre. Prend-on au piège
> La précipice, l'ombre et la bise et la neige ?
> Signe-t-on des marchés dans lesquels il soit dit
> Que l'Orteler s'enrôle et devient un bandit ?
> Quel poing cyclopéen, dites, ô roches noires,
> Pourra briser la Dent de Morcle en vos mâchoires ?
> Quel assembleur de bœufs pourra forger un joug
> Qui du pic de Glaris aille au piton de Zoug ?
> C'est naturellement que les monts sont fidèles
> Et purs, ayant la forme âpre des citadelles,
> Ayant reçu de Dieu des créneaux où, le soir,
> L'homme peut, d'embrasure en embrasure, voir
> Étinceler le fer de lance des étoiles.
> Est-il une araignée, aigle, qui dans ses toiles
> Puisse prendre la trombe et la rafale et toi ?
> Quel chef recrutera le Salève ? à quel roi
> Le Mythen dira-t-il : ' Sire, je vais descendre ! '
> Qu'après avoir dompté l'Athos, quelque Alexandre,
> Sorte de héros monstre aux cornes de taureau,
> Aille donc relever sa robe à la Jungfrau !

Comme la vierge, ayant l'ouragan sur l'épaule,
Crachera l'avalanche à la face du drôle !
.   .   .   .

Non, rien n'est mort ici.   Tout grandit, et s'en vante.
L'Helvétie est sacrée, et la Suisse est vivante ;
Ces monts sont des héros et des religieux ;
Cette nappe de neige aux plis prodigieux
D'où jaillit, lorsqu'en mai la tiède brise ondoie,
Toute une floraison folle d'air et de joie,
Et d'où sortent des lacs et des flots murmurants,
N'est le linceul de rien, excepté des tyrans.

This glorious poem of the first series finds a glorious echo
in the twenty-fifth division of the second ; even as the Pyre-
nean cycle which opened in the first series is brought in
the second to fuller completion of equal and corresponsive
achievement.   It is wonderful, even in this vast world of
poetic miracle where nothing is other than wonderful, that
Masferrer should be equal to *Aymerillot* in frank majesty of
beauty ; that even after *Le Parricide* a fresh depth of tragic
terror should be sounded by *Gaïffer-Jorge* ; and that after
all he had already written on fatherhood and sonship, on
duty and chivalry, on penitence and pride, Victor Hugo
should have struck so new and so profound a note as rings
in every line of *La Paternité*.

But of all echoes and of all responses which reverberate
from end to end of these three great sections of song, the
very sweetest, and perhaps the very deepest, are those
evoked by love of little children and compassionate reverence for the poor.   If but one division were to be left us
out of all the second series, and fate or chance, comparatively compassionate in its cruelty, gave us our choice
which this one should be, the best judgments might perhaps

decide to preserve the twenty-third at all events. What the words 'realism' and 'naturalism' do naturally and really signify in matters of art, the blatant babblers who use them to signify the photography of all things abject might learn, if shallow insolence and unclean egotism were suddenly made capable of learning, by the study of only the two poems which set before us in two different forms the strength of weakness in the child whose love redeems his father from death and the child who can find no comfort but in death for the lack of a father's love. There is nothing in Homer, in Dante, or in Shakespeare, the three only poets who can properly be cited for comparison, of a pathos more poignant in its bitter perfection of sweetness.

Among the many good things which seem, for the lovers of poetry, to have come out of one and so great an evil as the long exile of Hugo from his country, there is none better or greater than the spiritual inhalation of breeze and brine into the very heart of his genius, the miraculous impregnation of his solitary Muse by the sea-wind. This influence could not naturally but combine with the lifelong influence of all noble sympathies to attract his admiration and his pity towards the poor folk of the shore, and to produce from that sense of compassion for obscurer sorrows and brotherhood with humbler heroism than his own such work as the poem which describes the charity of a fisherman's wife towards the children of her dead neighbour. It has all the beautiful precision and accurate propriety of detail which distinguish the finest idyls of Theocritus or Tennyson, with a fervour of pathetic and imaginative emotion which Theocritus never attained, and which Tennyson has attained but once. All the horror of death,

all the trouble and mystery of darkness, seem as we read
to pass into our fancy with the breath of pervading night,
and to vanish with the husband's entrance at sunrise before
the smile with which the wife draws back the curtains of
the cradle.

This poem, which so many hearts must have treasured
among their choicest memories for now so many years, has
found at length its fellow in the final volume of the book.
There is even more savour of the sea in the great lyric
landscape called *Les paysans au bord de la mer* than in the
idyllic interior called *Les pauvres gens*.   There we felt the
sea-wind and saw the sea-mist through the chinks of door
and window ; but here we feel all the sweep of the west
wind's wings, and see all the rush of rain along the stormy
shore that the flock of leaping waves has whitened with the
shreddings of their fleece.   We remember in *Les Voix
Intérieures* the all but matchless music of the song of the
sea-wind's trumpet, and in the notes of this new tune we
find at last that music matched and deepened and prolonged.   In the great lyric book which gives us the third of
the four blasts blown from *Les Quatre Vents de l'Esprit*,
there are visions as august and melodies as austere as this ;
but outside the vast pale of the master's work we should
look for the likeness of such songs in vain.   The key of all
its tenderness if not of all its terror is struck in these two
first verses.

> Les pauvres gens de la côte,
> L'hiver, quand la mer est haute
>   Et qu'il fait nuit,
> Viennent où finit la terre
> Voir les flots pleins de mystère
>   Et pleins de bruit.

> Ils sondent la mer sans bornes ;
> Ils pensent aux écueils mornes
> Et triomphants ;
> L'orpheline pâle et seule
> Crie : ô mon père ! et l'aïeule
> Dit : mes enfants !

The verses which translate the landscape are as absolutely incomparable in their line as those which render the emotion of the watchers. Witness this :—

> Et l'on se met en prières,
> Pendant que joncs et bruyères
> Et bois touffus,
> Vents sans borne et flots sans nombre,
> Jettent dans toute cette ombre
> Des cris confus.

Here, as usual, it is the more tragic aspect of the waters that would appear to have most deeply impressed the sense or appealed to the spirit of Victor Hugo. He seems to regard the sea with yet more of awe than of love, as he may be said to regard the earth with even more of love than of awe. He has put no song of such sweet and profound exultation, such kind and triumphant motherhood, into the speaking spirit of the sea as into the voice of the embodied earth. He has heard in the waves no word so bountiful and benignant as the message of such verses as these :—

> La terre est calme auprès de l'océan grondeur ;
> La terre est belle ; elle a la divine pudeur
> De se cacher sous les feuillages ;
> Le printemps son amant vient en mai la baiser ;
> Elle envoie au tonnerre altier pour l'apaiser
> La fumée humble des villages.

Ne frappe pas, tonnerre. Ils sonts petits, ceux-ci.
La terre est bonne ; elle est grave et sévère aussi ;
   Les roses sont pures comme elle ;
Quiconque pense, espère et travaille lui plaît ;
Et l'innocence offerte à tout homme est son lait,
   Et la justice est sa mamelle.

La terre cache l'or et montre les moissons ;
Elle met dans le flanc des fuyantes saisons
   Le germe des saisons prochaines,
Dans l'azur les oiseaux qui chuchotent : aimons !
Et les sources au fond de l'ombre, et sur les monts
   L'immense tremblement des chênes.

The loving loveliness of these divine verses is in sharp
contrast with the fierce resonance of those in which the sea's
defiance is cast as a challenge to the hopes and dreams of
mankind :—

Je suis la vaste mêlée,
Reptile, étant l'onde, ailée,
   Étant le vent ;
Force et fuite, haine et vie,
Houle immense, poursuivie
   Et poursuivant

The motion of the sea was never till now so perfectly
done into words as in these three last lines ; but anyone to
whom the water was as dear or dearer than the land at its
loveliest would have found a delight as of love no less con-
ceivable than a passion as of hatred in the more visible and
active life of waves, and at least as palpable to the 'shaping
spirit of imagination.' It remains true, after all, for the
greatest as for the humblest, that—in the words of one of
the very few poets whose verses are fit to quote even after a
verse of Hugo's—

> we receive but what we give,
> And in our life alone doth nature live ;

so far, at least, as her life concerns us, and is perceptible or appreciable by our spirit or our sense. A magnificent instance of purely dramatic vision, in which the lyric note is tempered to the circumstance of the speakers with a kind of triumphant submission and severe facility, is *La Chanson des Doreurs de Proues*. The poet's unequalled and unapproached variety in mastery of metre and majesty of colour and splendid simplicity of style, no less exact than sublime, and no less accurate than passionate, could hardly be better shown than by comparison of the opening verses with the stanza cited above.

> Nous sommes les doreurs de proues.
> Les vents, tournant comme des roues,
> Sur la verte rondeur des eaux
> Mêlent les lueurs et les ombres,
> Et dans les plis des vagues sombres
> Traînent les obliques vaisseaux.
>
> La bourrasque décrit des courbes,
> Les vents sont tortueux et fourbes,
> L'archer noir souffle dans son cor,
> Ces bruits s'ajoutent aux vertiges,
> Et c'est nous qui dans ces prodiges
> Faisons rôder des spectres d'or.
>
> Car c'est un spectre que la proue.
> Le flot l'étreint, l'air la secoue ;
> Fière, elle sort de nos bazars
> Pour servir aux éclairs de cible,
> Et pour être un regard terrible
> Parmi les sinistres hasards.

It is more than fifty years since *Les Orientales* rose radiant upon the world of letters, and the hand which gave them to mankind has lost so little of its cunning that we are wellnigh tempted to doubt whether then, for all its skill and sureness of touch, it had quite the same strength and might of magnificent craftsmanship as now.   There was fire as well as music on the lips of the young man, but the ardour of the old man's song seems even deeper and keener than the passion of his past.   The fervent and majestic verses of June 2, 1883, strike at starting the note of measureless pity and immeasurable indignation which rings throughout the main part of the fifth and last volume almost louder and fuller, if possible, than it was wont.   All Victor Hugo, we may say, is in this book ; it is as one of those ardent evening skies in which sunrise and sunset seem one in the flush of overarching colour which glows back from the west to the east with reverberating bloom and fervour of rose-blossom and fire.   There is life enough in it, enough of the breath and spirit and life-blood of living thought, to vivify a whole generation of punier souls and feebler hearts with the heat of his fourscore years.   It may be doubted whether there ever lived a poet and leader of men to whom these glorious verses would be so closely applicable as to their writer.

> Un grand esprit en marche a ses rumeurs, ses houles,
> Ses chocs, et fait frémir profondément les foules,
> Et remue en passant le monde autour de lui.
> On est épouvanté si l'on n'est ébloui ;
> L'homme comme un nuage erre et change de forme ;
> Nul, si petit qu'il soit, échappe au souffle énorme ;
> Les plus humbles, pendant qu'il parle, ont le frisson.

Ainsi quand, évadé dans le vaste horizon,
L'aquilon qui se hâte et qui cherche aventure
Tord la pluie et l'éclair, comme de sa ceinture
Une fille défait en souriant le nœud,
Quand l'immense vent gronde et passe, tout s'émeut,
Pas un brin d'herbe au fond des ravins, que ne touche
Cette rapidité formidable et farouche.

And this wind ' bloweth where it listeth ' : now it comes
to us charged with all the heart of all the roses in the world ;
its breath when it blows towards Greece has in it a murmur
as of Shelley's *Epipsychidion* ; the caress of its love-making
has all the freedom and all the purity of Blake's ; now it
passes by us in darkness, from depth to depth of the bitter
mystery of night. A vision of ruined worlds, the floating
purgatorial prisons of ruined souls, adrift as hulks on the
sea of darkness everlasting, shows us the harvest in eternity
of such seed as was sown in time by the hands of such
guides and rulers of men as we hear elsewhere speaking
softly with each other in the shadows, within hail of the
confessional and the scaffold. The loftiest words of counsel
sound sweeter in the speech of this great spirit than the
warmest whispers of pleasure ; and again, the heaviest
stroke of damning satire is succeeded by the tenderest touch
of a compassion that would leave not a bird in captivity.
The hand that opens the cage-door is the same which has
just turned the key on the braggart swordsman, neither
' victorious ' nor ' dead,' but condemned to everlasting prison
behind the bars of iron verse.

But the two long poems which dominate the book, like
two twin summits clothed round with fiery cloud and crowned
with stormy sunshine, tower equal in height and mass of

structure with the stateliest in the two parts preceding. The voice that rolls throughout *Les Quatre Jours d'Elciis* the thunder of its burning words reawakens and prolongs the echo of Félibien's pity and wrath over the murdered corpse of a child unborn ; we recognise in the speaker a kinsman of Welf's, the unconquerable old castellan of Osbor, delivered only by an act of charity into the treacherous hands of the princes whom his citadel had so long defied. Of Elciis, as of him, the poet might have said—

> Si la mer prononçait des noms dans ses marées,
> O vieillard, ce serait des noms comme le tien.

Such names will no doubt provoke the soft superior smile of a culture too refined for any sort of enthusiasm but the elegant ecstasy of self-worship ; and such simplicity will excite, on the other hand, a deep-mouthed bray of scorn from the whole school or church whose apostle in France was St. Joseph de Maistre, in England St. Thomas Coprostom, late of Craigenputtock and Chelsea ; the literary lappers of imaginary blood, the inkhorn swordsmen and spokesmen of immaterial iron. The rage of their contempt for such as Hugo, the loathing of their scorn for such as Shelley, ought long since to have abashed the believers in principles which find no abler defenders or more effective champions than these.

For it is true that the main truths preached and enforced and insisted on by such fanatical rhetoricians as Milton, as Mazzini, or as Hugo, are as old as the very notion of right and wrong, as the rudest and crudest conception of truth itself ; and it is undeniable that the Gospel according to St. Coprostom has the invaluable merit of pungent eccentricity and comparatively novel paradox. The evangelist of 'golden silence'—whose own speech, it may be admitted, was 'quite other' than 'silvern'—is logically justified in his blatant but ineffable contempt for the dull old doctrines of mere mercy and righteousness, of liberty that knows no higher law than duty, of duty that depends for its existence on the existence of liberty. Such a creed, in the phrase of a brother philosopher whose 'reminiscences' may be gathered from Shakespeare, and whose views of his contemporaries were identical in tone and expression with the opinions of Mr. Carlyle on his, was mouldy before our grandsires had nails on their toes. It is far more intelligent, more original, more ingenious than all the old cant and rant against priests and kings and vowbreakers and blood-spillers, to discover the soul of goodness in Ratbert the Second or Napoleon the Third, and observingly distil it out into analytic and monodramatic blank verse. And it will never be said that this reaction against the puerile or senile preference of right to wrong and principle to prosperity has not been carried far enough in our time. Carlyle, the man of brass, and Musset, the man of clay, as far apart on all other points as two writers of genius could well be, have shown themselves at one in high-souled scorn for 'principles of mere rebellion' such as Landor's and Milton's, or for such 'belief in a new Brutus' as might disturb the dream of Augustulus. But, even as an old paradox becomes with time a commonplace, so does an old commonplace become in its turn a paradox; and a generation whose poets and historians have long blown the trumpet before the legitimacy of Romanoffs or the bastardy of Bonapartes may properly be startled and scandalized at the childish eccentricity of an old-world idealist who

maintains his obsolete and preposterous belief that massacre
is murder, that robbery is theft, and that perjury is treason.
No newer doctrine, no sounder philosophy, no riper wisdom
than this, can be gathered from the declamations of those
idle old men—as Goneril, for example, would have called
them—who speak this poet's mind again and again in verse
which has no more variety of splendour or magnificence of
music than the sea.

> Hélas, on voit encor les astres se lever,
> L'aube sur l'Apennin jeter sa clarté douce,
> L'oiseau faire son nid avec des brins de mousse,
> La mer battre les rocs dans ses flux et reflux,
> Mais la grandeur des cœurs c'est ce qu'on ne voit plus.

There is nothing ingenious in that ; it is no better, intel-
lectually considered, than a passage of Homer or Isaiah.

But though every verse has the ring of tested gold, and
every touch gives notice of the master's hand, yet the glory
even of these *Four Days* is eclipsed by the *Vision of Dante*.
Far apart and opposite as they stand in all matters of poetic
style and method—Dante writing with the rigid and reserved concision of a Tacitus, Hugo with the rushing yet
harmonious profusion of a Pindar—the later master is the
only modern poet who could undertake without absurdity or
presumption to put words worthy of Dante into Dante's
mouth.   The brazen clatter of Byron's *Prophecy* was not redeemed or brought into tune by the noble energy and sound
insight of the political sympathies expressed in the accent
of a stump-orator to the tune of a barrel-organ.   But a verse
of Hugo's falls often as solid and weighty and sure, as full
in significance of perfect and pregnant sound, as even a

verse of Alighieri's.   He therefore, but he alone, had the
power and the right to call up the spirit of Dante now thirty
years ago, and bid it behold all the horrors of Europe in
1853 ; the Europe of Haynau and Radetzky, of Nicholas
the First and Napoleon the Last.   Any great modern poet's
notion of an everlasting hell must of course be less merely
material than Dante's mechanism of hot and cold circles,
fire and ice, ordure and mire ; but here is the same absolute
and equitable assent to justice, the same fierce and ardent
fidelity to conscience, the same logic and the same loyalty
as his.

> O sentence ! ô peine sans refuge !
> Tomber dans le silence et la brume à jamais !
> D'abord quelque clarté des lumineux sommets
> Vous laisse distinguer vos mains désespérées.
> On tombe, on voit passer des formes effarées,
> Bouches ouvertes, fronts ruisselants de sueur,
> Des visages hideux qu'éclaire une lueur.
> Puis on ne voit plus rien.   Tout s'efface et recule.
> La nuit morne succède au sombre crépuscule.
> On tombe.   On n'est pas seul dans ces limbes d'en bas ;
> On sent frissonner ceux qu'on ne distingue pas ;
> On ne sait si ce sont des hydres ou des hommes ;
> On se sent devenir les larves que nous sommes ;
> On entrevoit l'horreur des lieux inaperçus,
> Et l'abîme au-dessous, et l'abîme au-dessus.
> Puis tout est vide ! on est le grain que le vent sème.
> On n'entend pas le cri qu'on a poussé soi-même ;
> On sent les profondeurs qui s'emparent de vous ;
> Les mains ne peuvent plus atteindre les genoux ;
> On lève au ciel les yeux et l'on voit l'ombre horrible ;
> On est dans l'impalpable, on est dans l'invisible ;
> Des souffles par moments passent dans cette nuit.
> uis on ne sent plus rien.—Pas un vent, pas un bruit,

> Pas un souffle ; la mort, la nuit ; nulle rencontre ;
> Rien, pas même une chute affreuse ne se montre :
> Et l'on songe à la vie, au soleil, aux amours,
> Et l'on pense toujours, et l'on tombe toujours !

The resurrection of the victims to give evidence at the summons of the archangel—a heavy cloud of witnesses,

> Triste, livide, énorme, ayant un air de rage—

men bound to the yoke like beasts, women with bosoms gashed by the whip, children with their skulls cleft open—is direful as any less real and actual vision of the elder hell.

> Les cris d'enfant surtout venaient à mon oreille ;
> Car, dans cette nuit-là, gouffre où l'équité veille,
> La voix des innocents sur toute autre prévaut,
> C'est le cri des enfants qui monte le plus haut,
> Et le vagissement fait le bruit du tonnerre.

The appeal for justice which follows, with its enumeration of horrors unspeakable except by history and poetry, is followed in its turn by the evocation of the soldiers whom this army of martyrs has with one voice designated to the angel of judgment as their torturers and murderers. The splendid and sonorous verses in which the muster of these legions after legions, with their garments rolled in blood, is made to defile before the eyes of reader or hearer, can be matched only by the description of the Swiss mercenaries in *Le Régiment du baron Madruce.*

> Un grand vautour doré les guidait comme un phare.
> Tant qu'ils étaient au fond de l'ombre, la fanfare,
> Comme un aigle agitant ses bruyants ailerons,
> Chantait claire et joyeuse au front des escadrons,

Trompettes et tambours sonnaient, et des centaures
Frappaient des ronds de cuivre entre leurs mains sonores ;
Mais, dès qu'ils arrivaient devant le flamboiement,
Les clairons effarés se taisaient brusquement,
Tout ce bruit s'éteignait.   Reculant en désordre,
Leurs chevaux se cabraient et cherchaient à les mordre,
Et la lance et l'épée échappaient à leur poing.

Challenged to make answer, the assassins of Italy and Hungary plead that they were but the sword, their captains were the hand.   These are summoned in their turn, and cast their crimes in turn upon the judges who bade them shed blood and applauded their bloodshedding in the name of law and justice.   And the judges and lawgivers are summoned in their stead.

Ces hommes regardaient l'ange d'un air surpris :
Comme, en lettres de feu, rayonnait sur sa face
Son nom, Justice, entre eux ils disaient à voix basse :
Que veut dire ce mot qu'il porte sur son front ?

Charged with their complicity in all the public crime and shame and horror of their period, these in turn cast the burden of their wrong-doing on the princes who commanded them and they obeyed, seeing how the priests and soothsayers had from all time assured them that kings were the images of God.   The images of God are summoned, and appear, in the likeness of every form of evil imaginable by man.

Devant chaque fantôme, en la brume glacée,
Ayant le vague aspect d'une croix renversée,
Venait un glaive nu, ferme et droit dans le vent,
Qu'aucun bras ne tenait et qui semblait vivant.

Strange shapes of winged and monstrous beasts were harnessed to the chariots on which the thrones of the earth were borne forward. The figure seated on the last of them will be recognisable beyond all possibility of mistake by any reader whose eyes have ever rested on a face which beyond most human faces bore the visible image and superscription of the soul behind it.

> Les trônes approchaient sous les lugubres cieux ;
> On entendait gémir autour des noirs essieux
> La clameur de tous ceux qu'avaient broyés leurs roues ;
> Ils venaient, ils fendaient l'ombre comme des proues ;
> Sous un souffle invisible ils semblaient se mouvoir ;
> Rien n'était plus étrange et plus farouche à voir
> Que ces chars effrayants tourbillonnant dans l'ombre.
> Dans le gouffre tranquille où l'humanité sombre,
> Ces trônes de la terre apparaissaient hideux.
>
> Le dernier qui venait, horrible au milieu d'eux,
> Était à chaque marche encombré de squelettes
> Et de cadavres froids aux bouches violettes,
> Et le plancher rougi fumait, de sang baigné ;
> Le char qui le portait dans l'ombre était traîné
> Par un hibou tenant dans sa griffe une hache.
> Un être aux yeux de loup, homme par la moustache,
> Au sommet de ce char s'agitait étonné,
> Et se courbait furtif, livide et couronné.
> Pas un de ces césars à l'allure guerrière
> Ne regardait cet homme. A l'écart, et derrière,
> Vêtu d'un noir manteau qui semblait un linceul,
> Espèce de lépreux du trône, il venait seul ;
> Il posait les deux mains sur sa face morose
> Comme pour empêcher qu'on y vît quelque chose ;
> Quand parfois il ôtait ses mains en se baissant,
> En lettres qui semblaient faites avec du sang
> On lisait sur son front ces trois mots :—Je le jure.

It is a fearful thing, said the Hebrew, to fall into the hands of the living God ; and it is a fearful thing for a male-factor to fall into the hands of an ever-living poet. The injured Cæsars of Rome—Tiberius, for example, and Domitian—have not even yet been delivered by the most conscientious efforts of German and Anglo-German Cæsarists out of the prison whose keys are kept by Juvenal ; and a greater than Juvenal is here.

Summoned to make answer to the charge of the angel of judgment, even these also have their resource for evasion, and cast all their crimes upon the Pope.

> Il nous disait : Je suis celui qui parle aux rois ;
> Quiconque me résiste et me brave est impie.
> Ce qu'ici-bas j'écris, là-haut Dieu le copie.
> L'église, mon épouse, éclose au mont Thabor,
> A fait de la doctrine une cage aux fils d'or,
> Et comme des oiseaux j'y tiens toutes les âmes.

This man had blessed the murderers in their triumph, and cursed their victims in the grave :—

> Sa ceinture servait de corde à nos potences.
> Il liait de ses mains l'agneau sous nos sentences ;
> Et quand on nous criait : Grâce ! il nous criait : Feu !
> C'est à lui que le mal revient. Voilà, grand Dieu,
> Ce qu'il a fait : voilà ce qu'il nous a fait faire.
> Cet homme était le pôle et l'axe de la sphère ;
> Il est le responsable et nous le dénonçons !
> Seigneur, nous n'avons fait que suivre ses leçons,
> Seigneur, nous n'avons fait que suivre son exemple.

And the pontiff whose advent and whose promises had been hailed with such noble trust and acclaimed with such noble thankfulness by those who believed in him as a

deliverer—by Landor among others, and by Hugo himself—
the Caiaphas-Iscariot whose benediction had consecrated
massacre and anointed perjury with the rancid oil of mal-
odorous gladness above its fellows in empire and in crime—
is summoned out of darkness to receive sentence by the
sevenfold sounding of trumpets.

> Vêtu de lin plus blanc qu'un encensoir qui fume,
> Il avait, spectre blême aux idoles pareil,
> Les baisers de la foule empreints sur son orteil,
> Dans sa droite un bâton comme l'antique archonte,
> Sur son front la tiare, et dans ses yeux la honte.
> De son cou descendait un long manteau doré,
> Et dans son poignet gauche il tenait, effaré,
> Comme un voleur surpris par celui qu'il dérobe,
> Des clefs qu'il essayait de cacher sous sa robe.
> Il était effrayant à force de terreur.
>
> Quand surgit ce vieillard, on vit dans la lueur
> L'ombre et le mouvement de quelqu'un qui se penche.
> A l'apparition de cette robe blanche,
> Au plus noir de l'abîme un tonnerre gronda.

Then from all points of the immeasurable spaces, from
the womb of the cloud and the edge of the pit, is witness
given against Pope Pius IX. by the tyrants and the victims,
mothers and children and old men, the judges and the
judged, the murderers mingling with the murdered, great and
small, obscure and famous.

> Tous ceux que j'avais vus passer dans les ténèbres,
> Avançant leur front triste, ouvrant leur œil terni,
> Fourmillement affreux qui peuplait l'infini,
> Tous ces spectres, vivant, parlant, riant naguère,
> Martyrs, bourreaux, et gens du peuple et gens de guerre,

Regardant l'homme blanc d'épouvante ébloui,
Élevèrent la main et crièrent : C'est lui.

Et pendant qu'ils criaient, sa robe devint rouge.

Au fond du gouffre où rien ne tressaille et ne bouge
Un écho répéta :—C'est lui !—Les sombres rois
Dirent :—C'est lui ! c'est lui ! c'est lui ! voilà sa croix !
Les clefs du paradis sont dans ses mains fatales.—
Et l'homme-loup, debout sur les cadavres pâles
Dont le sang tiède encor tombait dans l'infini,
Cria d'une voix rauque et sourde :—Il m'a béni !

A judgment less terrible than what follows is that by
which Dante long ago made fast the gates of hell upon
Nicholas and Boniface and Clement with one stroke of his
inevitable hand.   The ghastly agony of the condemned is
given with all the bitterest realism of the great elder anti-
papist who sent so many vicars of Christ to everlasting
torment for less offences than those of Mastai-Ferretti.

Lui se tourna vers l'ange en frissonnant,
Et je vis le spectacle horrible et surprenant
D'un homme qui vieillit pendant qu'on le regarde.
L'agonie éteignit sa prunelle hagarde,
Sa bouche bégaya, son jarret se rompit,
Ses cheveux blanchissaient sur son front décrépit,
Ses tempes se ridaient comme si les années
S'étaient subitement sur sa face acharnées,
Ses yeux pleuraient, ses dents claquaient comme au gibet
Les genoux d'un squelette, et sa peau se plombait,
Et, stupide, il baissait, à chaque instant plus pâle,
Sa tête qu'écrasait la tiare papale.

From the sentence passed upon him after the avowal
extorted by the angel of doom that he has none in the

world above him but God alone on whom to cast the re-
sponsibility of his works, not a word may be taken away for
the purpose of quotation, as not a word could have been
added to it by Dante or by Ezekiel himself. But about the
eternity of his damnation there is not, happily for the human
conscience, any manner of doubt possible ; it must endure
as long as the poem which proclaims it : in other words, as
long as the immortality of poetry itself.

This great and terrible poem, the very crown or copingstone of all the *Châtiments*, has a certain affinity with two
others in which the poet's yearning after justice and mercy
has borne his passionate imagination as high and far as here.
In *Sultan Mourad* his immeasurable and incomparable
depth of pity and charity seems wellnigh to have swallowed
up all sense of necessary retribution : it is perhaps because
the portentous array of crimes enumerated is remote in
time and place from all experience of ours that conscience
can allow the tenderness and sublimity of its inspiration to
justify the moral and ratify the sentence of the poem :—

> Viens ! tu fus bon un jour, sois à jamais heureux.
> Entre, transfiguré ! tes crimes ténébreux,
> O roi, derrière toi s'effacent dans les gloires ;
> Tourne la tête, et vois blanchir tes ailes noires.

But in the crowning song of all the great three cycles
every need and every instinct of the spirit may find the
perfect exaltation of content. The vast and profound sense
of ultimate and inevitable equity which animates every line
of it is as firm and clear as the solid and massive splendour
of its articulate expression. The date of it is outside and
beyond the lapse of the centuries of time ; but the rule of

the law of righteousness is there more evident and indisputable than ever during the flight of these. Hardly in the Hebrew prophecies is such distinct and vivid sublimity, as of actual and all but palpable vision, so thoroughly impregnated with moral and spiritual emotion. Not a verse of all that strike root into the memory for ever but is great alike by imagination and by faith. In such a single line as this—

> Que qui n'entendit pas le remords l'entendrait—

there is the very note of conscience done into speech, cast into form, forged into substance

> Avec de l'équité condensée en airain.

But this couplet, for immensity of imaginative range, is of one birth with the sublimest verses in the Book of Job :—

> Et toute l'épouvante éparse au ciel est sœur
> De cet impénétrable et morne avertisseur.

From the magnificent overture to the second series, in which the poet has embodied in audible and visible symbol the vision whence this book was conceived—a vision so far surpassing the perhaps unconsciously imitative inspiration of the Apocalypse, with its incurably lame and arduously prosaic efforts to reproduce the effect or mimic the majesty of earlier prophecies, that we are amazed if not scandalized to find that book actually bracketed in one sublime passage of this prelude with the greatest spiritual poem in the world, the Oresteia of Æschylus—the reader would infer that any student wishing to give a notion of the *Légende des Siècles* ought to have dwelt less than I have done upon a few of its innumerable beauties, and more than I have done upon the

impression of its incomparable grandeur.   But samples of
pure sweetness and beauty are more easily and perhaps
more profitably detached for quotation from their context
than samples of a sublimity which can only be felt by full
and appreciative study of an entire and perfect poem.   And
it is rather from the prelude itself than from any possible
commentary on it that a thoughtful and careful reader will
seek to gather the aim and meaning of the book.   It is
there likened to a vast disjointed ruin lit by gleams of
light—' le reste effrayant de Babel '—a palace and a charnel
in one, built by doom for death to dwell in :—

> Où se posent pourtant parfois, quand elles l'osent,
> De la façon dont l'aile et le rayon se posent,
> La liberté, lumière, et l'espérance, oiseau.

But over and within this book—

> traduit
> Du passé, du tombeau, du gouffre et de la nuit—

faith shines as a kindling torch, hope breathes as a quick-
ening wind, love burns as a cleansing fire.   It is tragic,
not with the hopeless tragedy of Dante or the all but hopeless tragedy of Shakespeare.   Whether we can or cannot
share the infinite hope and inviolable faith to which the
whole active and suffering life of the poet has borne such
unbroken and imperishable witness, we cannot in any case
but recognise the greatness and heroism of his love for
mankind.   As in the case of Æschylus it is the hunger and
thirst after righteousness, the deep desire for perfect justice
in heaven as on earth, which would seem to assure the prophet's inmost heart of its final triumph by the prevalence of

wisdom and of light over all claims and all pleas established
or asserted by the children of darkness, so in the case of
Victor Hugo is it the hunger and thirst after reconciliation,
the love of loving-kindness, the master passion of mercy,
which persists in hope and insists on faith, even in face of
the hardest and darkest experience through which a nation
or a man can pass. When evil was most triumphant
throughout Europe, he put forth in a single book of verse,
published with strange difficulty against incredible impedi-
ments, such a protest as would entitle him to say, in the
very words he has given to the Olympian of old—

> Quand, dans le saint pæan par les mondes chanté,
> L'harmonie amoindrie avorte ou dégénère,
> Je rends le rhythme aux cieux par un coup de tonnerre :

and now more than ever would the verses that follow befit
the lips of their author, if speaking in his own person :—

> Mon crâne plein d'échos, plein de lueurs, plein d'yeux,
> Est l'antre éblouissant du grand Pan radieux ;
> En me voyant on croit entendre le murmure
> De la ville habitée et de la moisson mûre,
> Le bruit du gouffre au chant de l'azur réuni,
> L'onde sur l'océan, le vent dans l'infini,
> Et le frémissement des deux ailes du cygne.

It is held unseemly to speak of the living as we speak of
the dead ; when Victor Hugo has joined the company of
his equals, but apparently not till then, it will seem strange
to regard the giver of all the gifts we have received from
him with less than love that deepens into worship, than
worship that brightens into love. Meantime it is only in
the phrase of one of his own kindred, poet and exile and

prophet of a darker age than his, that the last word should here be spoken of the man by whose name our century will be known for ever to all ages and nations that keep any record or memory of what was highest and most memorable in the spiritual history of the past :—

Onorate l' altissimo poeta.